International Federation of Library Associations and Institutions
Fédération Internationale des Associations de Bibliothécaires et des Bibliothèques
Internationaler Verband der bibliothekarischen Vereine und Institutionen
Международная Федерация Библиотечных Ассоциаций и Учреждений

IFLA Publications 27

Dennis D. McDonald
Eleanor J. Rodger
and
Jeffrey L. Squires

International Study of Copyright of Bibliographic Records in Machine-Readable Form

A Report prepared for the International Federation of Library Associations and Institutions

K·G·Saur München · New York · London · Paris 1983

IFLA Publications
edited by Willem R. H. Koops

Recommended catalog entry:

McDonald, Dennis D.
International study of copyright
of bibliographic records in machine-
readable form / a report prepared for
the International Federation of Li-
brary Associations and Institutions;
by Dennis D. McDonald, Eleanor J. Rodger
and Jeffrey L. Squires. – New York etc.:
K. G. Saur, 1983. – 149 p.; 21 cm. –
(IFLA Publications; 27)
ISBN 3-598-20393-4

CIP-Kurztitelaufnahme der Deutschen Bibliothek

MacDonald, Dennis D.:
International study of copyright of bibliographic
records in machine-readable form : a report pre-
pared for the Internat. Fed. of Library Assoc. and
Institutions / Dennis D. McDonald, Eleanor J. Rodger
and Jeffrey S. Squires. – München ; New York ;
London ; Paris : Saur, 1983.
(IFLA publications ; 27)
ISBN 3-598-20393-4

NE: Rodger, Eleanor J.:; Squires, Jeffrey L.:;
International Federation of Library Associations
and Institutions: IFLA publications

ISSN 0344-6891 (IFLA publications)

Printed and bound in the Federal Republic of Germany
for K. G. Saur Verlag KG, München
by Hain Druck GmbH, Meisenheim/Glan

ISBN 3-598-20393-4

Table of Contents

Appendices

Introduction

The goal of the International Federation of Library Associations and Institutions (IFLA) program of Universal Bibliographic Control (UBC) is to have (1) the bibliographic description of a country's national imprints produced by the national bibliographic agency in that country in accordance with international standards and (2) free flow of these records among national agencies, in order to build towards more cost effective national library systems.

In the last decade, the technology has increased the potential for the interchange of bibliographic data. This has resulted in the evolving International MARC network whereby national agencies have implemented their own national MARC systems and are already involved in data interchange.

In recent years, many complex issues related to machine-readable data exchange have been brought to light, e.g. copyright, third party use, transborder data flow, etc. IFLA thought it would be useful to begin to consider these issues and requested funding from the Council on Library Resources (CLR) to address those having to do with copyright of bibliographic descriptions in machine-readable form. CLR generously supported the IFLA request and IFLA subsequently contracted with King Research, Inc. to perform the study.

The final report was submitted by King Research, Inc. to IFLA in May, 1982. Since that time, the Conference of Directors of National Libraries' International MARC Network Study: Steering Committee (IMNS:SC) and the Standing Committee of the Section of Information Technology have reviewed and commented on the report.

Work within IFLA is still in progress to determine if there should be a follow-on study and if so, on what topic(s). Although IFLA does not necessarily agree with all of the recommendations made by King Research, Inc., it was decided to make the report available at this time as written, in the interest of disseminating the information to the library community.

Additional comments by the readers of the report would be welcome. Such comments should be sent to IFLA Headquarters, P.O.B. 95312, 2509 CH, The Hague, Netherlands.

Henriette D. Avram, Chairman
IFLA Professional Board

Preface

Following our submission of the first draft of this report to IFLA, we received several very useful comments and criticisms which we wish to address in this preface. The reader should be aware of these when reading the report so that the applicability of the findings to his or her own situation can be assessed.

First, the study has a noticeable North American bias in terms of the individuals who were interviewed and in terms of the literature which was reviewed. While this is partially due to time and budget constraints, we admit that our initial perception was that many of the issues which generated this study are true on both national and international levels. Bibliographic utilities in the U.S. have, for example, struggled with the issue of record ownership. While the study does have a North American bias, however, we are not yet convinced that any of our major findings would have changed significantly had more national representatives been contacted for their personal views. However, we must rely upon the reader to judge the validity of this perception.

Second, we concentrated primarily upon the exchange of bibliographic data among the national bibliographic agencies themselves, mainly because this was the study topic of most direct concern to IFLA. The reader should note that another area of concern is the re-distribution of bibliographic data by parties after they obtain copies of data from the national bibliographic agencies. As the reader will note when reading the report, we raise several serious practical questions concerning the utility of copyright law for governing the exchange of bibliographic data among the national agencies themselves. While we have not directly addressed the question of "third party" distribution, especially distribution by commercial organizations, we must entertain the possibility, suggested to us by one of this report's reviewers, that copyright law is a potentially useful method for attempting control of such distribution. We agree in principle with this particular viewpoint. But note our own perception that some of the practical limitations of using copyright law to control exchange between national agencies might still apply to third party distribution. Our main concern is the problem of monitoring and/or controlling the exchange of data among parties whose social and economic motives may differ substantially, even within the same country.

We can foresee circumstances, for example, where users of commercially-supplied bibliographic data may seek protection associated with their not-for-profit status, not unlike the "fair use" interpretations which are applied to selected instances of photocopying in the United States. Likewise, we can foresee instances in which some database producers may choose *not* to seek copyright protection. Perhaps most important, however, is that bibliographic data, because it plays a relatively small part in overall data transmissions and communication, may have to take a "back seat" compared with changes in national and international copyright laws and agreements.

Third, we note that this report concentrates, as planned and required, on bibliographic data. The reader should be aware that some of the concerns expressed here are not necessarily the same as those associated with computer software protection. For example, the Software Protection Committee of the Association of Data Processing Service Organizations (ADAPSO) has developed specific proposals for the improved protection of computer software; these include a consideration of the international (chiefly UCC) implications of such changes. (See Software Protection Committee, *A Proposal for the Improved Protection of Software.* Arlington, Virginia: Association of Data Processing Service Organizations, April 1982.)

Finally, we wish to emphasize that, even though our report raises several questions concerning the feasibility of using current copyright protection to control the exchange of data among national bibliographic agencies, we remain committed to the belief that copyright law must continue to be pursued nationally and internationally to help protect intellectual property, irrespective of whether such concerns are based on moral or economic grounds. No matter how difficult the issues surrounding legal protection of machine-readable databases, world dependence upon such databases as important components of international communication is bound to increase in the coming years. This is particularly true due to the increasing role of networks and bibliographic utilities which have the power to manipulate and distribute data initially supplied by a wide variety of commercial, national, and international agencies. Copyright law should not be viewed as a hindrance to communication. Instead, we hope that it will continue to be viewed as a method for ensuring that creators and owners of intellectuall property have adequate legal recourse to protect their intellectual and financial investments.

Dennis D. McDonald, Ph.D.
Project Director
May 1982

Acknowledgements

Many individuals and organizations have made significant contributions to this study.

We would like to acknowledge the staff of national bibliographic agencies worldwide who responded to our detailed survey questionnaire. We were extremely pleased by the response generated by this survey and hope that the results embodied in this report justify the substantial time and energy devoted by them to responding.

We would like to acknowledge the thoughts shared with us by the U.S. experts whom we contacted regarding this study for personal and telephone interviews. Their insight contributed substantially to a clarification of the issues dealt with in this study.

We would like to acknowledge the critical comments and encouragement supplied by Henriette Avram of the Library of Congress, whose understanding of the issues and the background of this study contributed substantially to its completion. We would also like to thank Michael Keplinger of the U.S. Copyright Office who contributed his comments throughout this project.

Thanks are also due to Hope E. A. Clement and Rodrick Duschesne of the National Library of Canada for their comments and suggestions.

We would also like to acknowledge the substantial contribution made by Mr. Jeffrey Squires, our legal consultant. In addition to the chapter reviewing the copyright law, Mr. Squires contributed substantively to all study phases.

We wish to thank IFLA and its steering group whose comments, guidance, and patience have been so helpful. Ms. Margreet Wijnstroom and Mr. A. L. van Wesemael of IFLA were very helpful. Dorothy Anderson, Director of the IFLA International Office for UBC was very thorough in her review of study materials and quick to respond to our requests for assistance. Finally, we hereby acknowledge Dr. Warren J. Haas and the Council on Library Resources for the support it provided for this project.

Dennis D. McDonald, Ph.D.
Project Director

SECTION 1
FINDINGS & RECOMMENDATIONS

1.1 Summary

We have examined copyright law and its implications for controlling the international exchange of bibliographic data in machine-readable form among national bibliographic agencies. We have found that copyright law at the present time does not provide a consistent and universal control mechanism to govern the international exchange of bibliographic data by these agencies. First, only a small number of national bibliographic agencies claim copyright protection for the machine-readable bibliographic records which they produce. Second, we have found that shortcomings exist concerning the law's direct applicability to the primarily non-commercial sharing of data among the national bibliographic agencies. These shortcomings are due both to the activities engaged in by the national bibliographic agencies which actively promote sharing as well as to the uncertainties concerning the applicability of copyright law, both nationally and internationally, to individual computerized bibliographic records.

We conclude that the most feasible mechanisms which exist at the present time for governing the international exchange of machine readable bibliographic data among national bibliographic agencies are bilateral exchange agreements which spell out in detail the types of uses which the parties to exchange are allowed to make of the exchanged data. Furthermore, we recommend that exchange partners not focus exclusively on copyright concerns but also on the economics and policy implications of their provision of machine-readable data to other organizations.

1.2 Discussion & Recommendations

This study was undertaken with an assumption that its primary focus would be copyright and its applicability to the control of the international exchange of bibliographic records in machine-readable form. During the course of the study we found that this focus was too narrow. Copyright, we found, is not the only uncertainty which exists regarding the international exchange of bibliographic records. Neither is the question of "record ownership" which has been debated substantially in the U.S., particularly regarding the sharing of bibliographic data by major bibliographic utilities. Rather, we found the greatest uncertainty to be a lack of appreciation of the economic realities involved in the production and exchange of bibliographic records in machine-readable form. It is our perception, based on our interviews, survey responses, and reading of the literature that the exchange of bibliographic data in machine-readable form has developed as an outgrowth of librarians' traditional professional responsibility and preference for the development of mechanisms to support the "free flow"* and exchange of information. This flow of information, as facilitated by computer technology, is an increasingly international business which is actively promoted by organizations and programs such as IFLA and Universal Bibliographic Control.

This exchange of data must, we feel, be encouraged to continue. Yet financial pressures on producing agencies will continue to increase as demand increases and as more agencies develop the capabilities for providing online access.

It may be inevitable that national agencies will turn increasingly to user charges as a means of recovering some of the costs of production and/or distribution. Alternatively, national agencies may seek to restrict access to their records if they find this warranted by increasing costs.

---

*We note here that "free flow" can take two meanings, the first being "free of cost" and the second being "free of impediments other than costs".

As we noted above, copyright was at first the primary focus of this study. Yet we have found that only a small number of agencies seek copyright protection for the systems of bibliographic records which they produce. While this may be due partly to a lack of clarity within various countries concerning copyright's applicability to bibliographic records, or even to the substantial variation among different countries of their own copyright laws, we have some reason to question whether copyright will ever be clarified sufficiently or in such a manner as to answer completely questions which arise concerning the international exchange of bibliographic data.

This is not to say that copyright is totally irrelevant; far from it. We strongly urge organizations such as IFLA to aggressively support programs such as UNESCO's which seek to clarify guidelines for copyright's treatment of bibliographic records. However, we recommend that continued reliance also be placed on bilateral exchange agreements to govern bibliographic data exchange. An excellent beginning has already been made at developing such exchange agreements. However, we have found that it is unrealistic to think that a universal, standardized exchange agreement will exist which can be entered into automatically by exchange partners. This statement is based on the following factors:

1. Different agencies will have different reasons for entering into exchange agreements and will also differ as to the interests they wish to protect.

2. Agencies will differ as to the degree they must (or wish to) recover costs of database production and/or distribution.

3. Agencies will differ substantially as to the ratio of the total number of records distributed to the total number of records received and/or used.

4. Agencies will differ as to the types of uses they wish to allow of the data which they supply.

5. National bibliographic agencies will differ as to the types of agencies to which they will be willing to release their records.

These factors should not be considered to be barriers to exchange, but they could form the basis for the development of components of exchange agreements in which the rights and responsibilities of exchange partners are clearly spelled out.

We noted above that a major uncertainty in this situation is a lack of appreciation or understanding of the economic realities of international data exchange. This is not a criticism of the parties involved since the sharing of information is a strongly-valued professional goal of librarians worldwide. Yet librarians are becoming increasingly aware of the economic value of bibliographic databases. We feel that the value of such data, both in economic and non-economic terms, would be seriously underestimated if librarians focus too narrowly on the question of ownership of individual records. In our opinion, the value of bibliographic databases derives not only from the use or modification of individual records but also in the overall availability of entire databases which can be searched and used for a wide variety of purposes.

These issues would be much simplified if bibliographic records were used solely for in-house cataloging purposes. But our study has revealed that, now or in the future, records may also be used as a basis for input to machine-readable databases which are then redistributed to third parties whose use of such data might eventually compete with the product of the original, originating agency.

Based on our knowledge of copyright issues raised in other areas (e.g., photocopying, off-the-air taping of television or radio broadcasts, pirating of motion pictures and fabric design, etc.), we feel that it is highly unrealistic to suppose that bibliographic record producers can ever completely control the modification or redistribution of the records they supply to other agencies, no matter how specific the intentions which might be spelled out by the original exchange partners. Unauthorized duplication and access is bound to occur, even if electronic safeguards (as desired by many survey respondents) are implemented. It is perhaps an unpleasant fact that the only sure way to prevent unauthorized duplication is to refuse to enter into an exchange agreement in the first place. We share the desire of librarians worldwide that this does not occur, since such a situation may seriously hamper the goals of standardized, non-duplicative international bibliographic control.

We believe that an ideal system for governing international exchange would be one which balances the universal availability of bibliographic data with the (varying) economic and non-economic interests of those agencies which produce such data. We have already noted that copyright law is only one of the factors which must be considered for the protection of the moral and economic rights of authors. Other factors which should be balanced in this regard are the increasingly important questions concerning the international transmission, by wire, satellite, microwave, or other means, of numeric and non-numeric data, and also the sharing of data among representatives of developing countries.

One of our goals in this study was to evaluate a variety of mechanisms which were relevant for controlling the exchange of bibliographic data in machine-readable form. Accordingly, we asked national bibliographic agencies worldwide to indicate their support or opposition to a variety of control mechanisms, including:

- Changes in the bibliographic agency's national copyright law so that it directly addressed copyright of computer data bases.

- Limited or controlled access via exchange agreements with user or intermediary organizations.

- Compulsory licensing, which would result in organizations automatically being able to use bibliographic records upon payment of a fee set by an international organization.

- Blanket licensing, which would allow use of records based on payment of a flat fee, perhaps tied to the size or budget of the user organization.

- An international consortium which would be empowered to negotiate exchange agreements for member organizations.

- No control.

- o Electronic control so that only authorized users could search and/or copy bibliographic agencies' records.

The strongest support was given by survey respondents to:

- o Limited or controlled access via exchange agreements with user organizations.

- o Electronic controls.

- o Changes in countries' copyright laws.

Respondents showed the greatest opposition to the concept of no control over the exchange of bibliographic records, with agencies which claimed copyright protection being more likely to oppose the concept of no control than agencies which do not claim copyright protection.

The survey responses essentially bear out what we found in our legal analysis and in our personal and telephone interviews: copyright protection is not a complete answer to the question of how best to control exchange and/or use of machine-readable bibliographic records. The concept of bilateral exchange agreements (the approach currently being used by many agencies) is strongly supported. The fact that control over exchange or use is desired even by those agencies which do not currently claim copyright protection may, in fact, be cue to both a lack of understanding of copyright as well as to its lack of specific coverage in many countries of computerized data bases. Furthermore, the support for electronic controls is, we feel, evidence that agencies are concerned about the unauthorized use of their records by organizations other than the parties to exchange. Such electronic controls take increased importance when online searching of bibliographic data bases is consdiered. In practical terms, however, electronic controls (e.g., passwords, restricted access, etc.) cannot be exerted directly since most of the national bibliographic agencies do not themselves provide online access. Such electronic controls could become important if it were possible, for example, to restrict the total number of contributed records retrieved from a data base. The ability to do this, however, will vary greatly depending upon the technical capabilities of the organizations with which bibliographic data are exchanged.

The options of control via international consortia, blanket licenses, and compulsory licenses may not have been supported by survey respondents simply because it was not possible in the questionnaire to fully explain how such hypothetical mechanisms might operate. A key component of such mechanisms is that exchange partners relinquish some control over factors such as identification of customers, record use, and/or price-setting. We feel confident in concluding that record producers are somewhat reluctant to relinquish control over re-use, selling, or modification of their records. This is based not only on the survey responses themselves but also on a general reluctance of any producer of intellectual property to relinquish total control over that property, no matter how efficient the licensing or distribution mechanism might be. As evidence of this we cite the existence in the U.S. of past opposition to compulsory licensing in cable television as well as to the continued operation by many U.S. publishers of their own photocopying and reprint permissions departments despite the existence of such organizations as the Copyright Clearance Center. Furthermore, the effort required to set up universal international licensing arrangements or consortia may be hampered by substantial differences among various countries in their telecommunications, information, and import-export policies.

Given the above situation in which there appears to be a potential conflict between the desire of record producers to control the exchange and use of their records, and the desire of the different organizations to share their data, it is clear that a balance must be developed between the needs of producers and the needs of users. Such a balancing of different national and international interests can only occur if parties with potential differences can communicate and compromise in an organized, cooperative fashion. While we have concluded above that the most realistic short-term methods available are bilateral agreements which address the issues raised in this report, we feel that implementaiton of recommendations such as the following would contribute substantially to a continuation of the international exchange of bibliographic records in machine-readable form. We note that implementation of several of these recommendations would require the establishment of a permanent responsibility within an existing organization (e.g., the UBC office), or the establishment of permanent working groups (e.g., members of the Conference of Directors of National Libraries).

Recommendation 1

IFLA or some other international organization (see Recommendation 2 below) should sponsor a study of the economics of the production, distribution, and use of bibliographic records in machine-readable form. Such a study should seek to quantify the costs and benefits of such exchanges so that exchange partners can accurately assess their own economic interests.

Also, IFLA should continue to monitor the international exchange of bibliographic data via an annual or semiannual survey, perhaps modelled on the international survey conducted as part of this study. Such a regular statistical survey would contribute substantially to measuring the achievement of long-term goals such as international bibliographic control as well as the international availability of publications. Such functions have been proposed for the international MARC office. Such a study could attempt the measurement of the volume and types of uses being made of internationally-exchanged data.

Recommendation 2

IFLA should actively promote a knowledge and awareness among its member organizations of the national and international issues which form the broader framework in which the exchange of bibliographic data takes place. Such a program should not be limited to copyright or technology but should also collect and distribute information concerning important international issues such as trans-border data flow, access by developing countries, and the degree to which legal and political differences among nations affect their participation in exchange networks.

Furthermore, IFLA could take the lead in setting up an international consortium of public sector and private sector organizations to address legal, political, technological, and social issues touched upon by the international exchange of bibliographic data. Such a consortium should not be limited to IFLA member organizations but should also include participation by telecommunications suppliers, national information organizations, government agencies, professional societies representing information users, and publishers. Organizations and programs such as UNESCO, UBC, UAP, ISSN, and ISBN may provide the basis from which such an international consortium might be developed. Possibly the first step which might be taken to develop such a consortium would be the sponsorship of an international conference devoted to clarifying the political and economic interests of the different parties involved with international data exchange.

Recommendation 3

IFLA should consider conducting an informal study among its national bibliographic agencies to determine why they participate in the international exchange of bibliographic data and what they perceive to be the advantages and disadvantages of such cooperation. Such an informal study might also investigate whether or not national agencies would support the development of international guidelines for setting usage fees to help producing agencies recover costs of producing or distributing machine-readable bibliographic data. The goal of such a study would be to provide further information on how to best balance the interests of both producers and users of bibliographic data. The goal of such a study would be to provide further information on how to best balance the interests of both producers and users of bibliographic data. An adjunct to such a study might be an analysis of the methods currently used by private-sector database producers and distributor systems for cost recovery.

Recommendation 4

While we found that copyright law is only one of the factors involved in controlling the exchange of bibliographic data, we recommend that IFLA, either as an organization or through its constituent members, actively promote an awareness among national legislators or government representatives of the special concerns of libraries for promoting the fair and balanced exchange of machine-readable bibliographic records. This might be accomplished by participating in international organizations which discuss copyright law and the international exchange of intellectual property. Another method would be the development of either a position paper or an objective background document which could be given to government officials concerned with copyright law revision.

Recommendation 5

This study dealt primarily with the exchange of bibliographic data in machine-readable form. As noted later in this report, however, the true value of bibliographic records is associated with who uses them and for what purposes they are used. This value, which may be a primary driving force behind producers' desires to exert some degree of control over how they are used, has as a major component the facilitation of document access and delivery.

We have not investigated the relationship (political, economic, legal, or otherwise) between the copyright of bibliographic data and the copyright of the documents which they describe. But it is perhaps inevitable that these two aspects of copyright will become increasingly intertwined as national and international document delivery systems, facilitated by computer and telecommunications technology, develop. Therefore, we recommend that IFLA help establish a permanent working group, possibly composed of members of the Conference of Directors of National Libraries, whose responsibility it will be to monitor the development of internationally-operating document delivery systems and make recommendations to insure that the interest of bibliographic data producers are taken into account in their development and operation.

Recommendation 6

This study concludes that a single, uniform, exchange agreement is not feasible for governing the bilateral exchange of bibliographic data between national bibliographic agencies. Instead, it recommends that exchange parties enter into bilateral exchange agreements where their own particular situations and interests can be taken into account. This report discusses many of the issues which might be treated in such exchange agreements. It is recommended that IFLA prepare a multi-language brochure or pamphlet, to be distributed to national agencies, which synthesizes the issues discussed in this report which should be considered by national agencies when entering into exchange or distribution agreements.

SECTION 2

SUMMARY OF STUDY APPROACH

This study utilized three primary sources of data:

1. A survey of national bibliographic agencies.
2. Personal and telephone interviews, with knowledgeable individuals, primarily in the U.S.
3. Review of copyright law relevant to bibliographic databases.

The survey was conducted via mail using a mail questionnaire developed by King Research and distributed in Spring of 1981 to 37 national bibliographic agencies, identified for us by IFLA as most likely to have ongoing programs for the production of bibliographic records in machine-readable form. Agencies were mailed a cover letter and questionnaire (Appendix C) as well as a document describing study objectives (Appendix A). Responses were received from 21 agencies, the last being received by King Research in November, 1981 (Appendix B).

The interviews were conducted during Spring and Fall of 1981 with 20 individuals (Appendix D). These individuals were selected by King Research to represent a variety of interests, including both public sector and private sector organizations and individuals. Suggestions for individuals to interview were also received from IFLA as well as the Library of Congress. Most interviewees received a list of interview questions (Appendix E) as well as a copy of the Study Objectives document.

The legal review was conducted by Jeffrey L. Squires of Jaffe, Squires, and Foote, 1000 Potomac St., N.W., Washington, D.C. 20007. Mr. Squires also served as a reactor to other portions of this report.

Background documents, some of them supplied by IFLA, the British Library, the National Library of Canada, and the Library of Congress, were reviewed as input to all phases of the study (see bibliography, Appendix F).

SECTION 3

DISCUSSION OF LEGAL ISSUES SURROUNDING BIBLIOGRAPHIC DATA EXCHANGE AMONG NATIONAL BIBLIOGRAPHIC AGENCIES

3.1 Summary

In this section we present a discussion of the legal issues surrounding the exchange of bibliographic records in machine-readable form, primarily in terms of a discussion of the applicability of copyright law. We wish to emphasize here that our primary focus has been on the bibliographic records produced and distributed by organizations such as the national bibliographic agencies which were surveyed during the course of this project; some of the comments below, for example, are not applicable to commercial agencies which engage in record production and/or distribution for profit. Some of the main points made in this discussion of the legal issues are the following:

- The two aspects of computer systems over which legal controls are the most relevant for controlling the uses made of such systems are the information processed by the computer (the data base) and the instructions which control the processing of this information (the program).

- While reciprocal copyright agreements among countries involved in exchange exist (e.g., Berne Convention and the Universal Copyright Convention), the relevant laws among the various countries are not themselves uniform.

- The degree of protection afforded by individual countries' copyright laws over computerized data bases is highly speculative, and uncertain.

- The major concern of bibliographic data base producers is not ownership *per se* but access to and use, modification, or redistribution of their records. Such concerns are not well-suited to control by copyright, partly because copyright was never designed to function as a body of law governing relationships of parties seeking to control distribution of works to a limited audience.

- The copyrightable element in a fact compilation, such as a bibliographic data base, is the structural relationship of the collection of individual records. Agencies which contribute to such compilations make no real creative contribution to the structure of a pre-existing system.

- Creators of bibliographic records already have the power to grant or withhold access to their data by means of legal or contractual exchange agreements; the assertion of copyright is not necessary to make such agreements enforceable.

- Such contractual exchange agreements may not be sufficient to control the exchange of all types of bibliographic or nonbibliographic data, but they appear to be sufficient for now and the foreseeable future to govern the international sharing of bibliographic data among the national bibliographic agencies which were the subject of this study.

3.2 Discussion of Legal Issues

Introduction

The wealth of the bibliographic record compiled by the major bibliographic agencies, joined with the enormous capability of modern computer and communications technologies, have engendered new problems for the international community. As enormous stores of bibliographic information are compiled and become available instantaneously for tradiitonal and novel uses, the people and institutions that are both creators and beneficiaries of these developments must deal with the distribution of the newly abundant commodity. Distribution requires the exercise of lawful authority. So we struggle to understand the mechanisms of law that are employed in controlling the distribution of computerized data bases such as those used in the international exchange of information among libraries.

Responses to the survey giving rise to this report show what one would normally expect to be the case: the national agencies responsible for the development of bibliographic records in machine-readable form are concerned with the distribution and use of information which has been systematically compiled through their efforts and with their nations' financial support. Another way of saying this is that they are concerned with ways to control dissemination of information that has been made easily available due, at least in part, to their efforts and investment. The concerns of different national agencies and representatives vary; underlying their concern---whether their primary goal is unhindered access to all records, the creation of a mechanism permitting them to limit and charge for distribution of records from their nation's "catalogue", or a binding international compact among all MARC creators and users---is a belief that there is applicable "law" that must govern their efforts to control distribution.

The adequacy of copyright law to serve as the source of legal principles for ordering relationships of producers and users of MARC-type data is one issue that led to the initiation of this study. Copyright has traditionally determined rights of reproduction in artistic and literary works; moreover, copyright is familiar to those who are regularly involved with various aspects of sharing literature and information. Nine of the national agencies responding to this survey indicated that they claim copyright protection for their machine-readable bibliographic records, and seven indicated they did not. While there appears some uncertainty, or at least a lact of uniformity, in reliance on copyright, there is no uncertainty that the new means of reproduction and dissemination have drastically changed international communications and have confused the applicability of traditional legal principles.[1] This confusion has produced efforts to understand and systematize international sharing of information collected and distributed with computer technology.[2] It is possible, at least with regard to compilations of data such as with machine-readable bibliographic data bases, that people have struggled too hard to apply familiar legal principles---such as copyright---to problems that do not require complex legal contortions in order to create satisfactory relationships.

This section provides an overview of that law which may pertain, both at the domestic and international level, when efforts are made to control distribution of the information contained in computer data bases, such as various national agencies' bibliographic data bases. After briefly discussing computerized information systems in general, we will describe the specific nature of machine-readable bibliographic data bases, and raise questions whether producers of these systems and records can (or need to) rely on copyright as a source for asserting rights in their works. It is hoped that this will communicate a useful and concise understanding---and dispel some potential misconceptions about---the significance of "the law" in creating arrangements for sharing and obtaining access to these records as they are created and maintained by the respective national agencies.

---

[1]In the United States, for example, the National Commission on New Technological Uses of Copyrighted Works (CONTU) was created in 1975 to make recommendations for legislative treatment of the impact of technological advance on publishing and information distribution, when the United States Congress found the area too novel and complex for treatment in the then-pending Copyright Revision Legislation. See Final Report of CONTU (U.S.G.P.O. 1979).

[2]The IFLA organization sponsoring the current study project has, in the past few years, been associated with studies similarly intended to yield greater understanding of the problems involving creation of an international system for bibliographic data base sharing. See Wells, The International MARC Network: A Study for an International Bibliographic Data Network (IFLA International Office for UBC 1977).

Computerized Information Retrieval Systems

The distribution of information compiled in a computer data base occurs as a result of the operation of an automated system. Several elements contribute to the necessary ordering of such a system. These elements can give rise to a claim of ownership based on some form of property rights that could enable the system's proprietor to exert some control. Examples of control are whether to deny access to the system, to charge a fee for access, to condition the use of information obtained by such access, or to insist upon reciprocal treatments with users of the system. We have to identify these elements to focus our understanding of what law is applicable, and in what way it may be applied, by anyone wishing to exert some kind of control over access to and use of the information found in a machine-readable collection of bibliographic records.

Among the general elements of a typical computer information system which could conceivably yield to some claim of ownership allowing for control over dissemination of information through the system are the following, which do not all equally contribute to a proprietor's legal control over the information contained in and provided by the system:

- The computer machinery itself, including processing equipment, printers, and terminals

- The computer software, or program, containing encoded instructions which direct the computing capabilities of the machine to accomplish specific tasks

- The communications lines between computers and terminals that provide distant users with access to the information produced by the computing process

- The information itself, either the raw data that is stored in machine-usable form, or the specific information that is provided in response to a user's request to cull the raw data to obtain information meeting identified criteria.

Of these elements, two (the raw information processed by the system's operation, and the computer program) may be susceptible to the types of unique ownership claims that would enable a system proprietor to exert some control over uses made of the information in the system. The raw data in any computer information system is often contributed and organized, whether it be bibliographic information or the names of every citizen in a given country, by those who desire to satisfy certain information needs and wish to enhance capabilities to put that information to use. Computer programs are often created especially to perform specific functions with identified masses of data, and are often tailored to the needs of specific users.

The ownership of unique intellectual property rights in computer and communications equipment, on the other hand, is normally vested in commercial entities which have invested in development and production of computer and communications equipment that provide users with the technical capability of manipulating and transporting data. They may sell or lease their products to users, and they normally have no direct proprietary interest in access to and use of the specific information their equipment processes and conveys.

So in order to understand the ways in which proprietors and operators of machine-readable bibliographic data bases can control the use of the information their systems provide, we look at the data base and, perhaps, the software utilized in the system, and try to ascertain what kind of proprietary rights may be relied upon to control the distribution and use of the information in their system. At the same time, we can refer to some of the refinements in various national laws, and in the hazy area of international law, to help ascertain what types of legal relationships the proprietors of bibliographic records in machine-readable form can reasonably rely upon.

Legal Protection of Computer Data Bases and Computer Programs

The literature about legal protection for computer data bases and programs is vast and growing and treats numerous complexities of law with great and often repetitive detail. Much of this literature has little bearing on current practical problems of ownership and distribution of computerized stores of information.[3] We shall here sacrifice much detail for the sake of conciseness and, hopefully, understanding.

Protecting the Contents of Machine-readable Bibliographic Data Bases

Data bases are compilations of large amounts of discrete information about selected topics, organized to allow those who wish access to certain information to readily identify that information which might be useful. Data bases of bibliographic information have traditionally been published in union catalogues, which users consult to identify monographs or articles by subject matter, title or author. Legal control over such masses of information has typically been a relatively simple matter. Publishers of these volumes could claim copyrights in their books and there was little dispute over their entitlement to prevent others from duplicating these volumes.

It is basic, and must be understood, that copyright provides no rights against reproduction of the discrete facts contained in the individual records compiled in a bibliographic data base such as a MARC system. Copyright protects only against the unauthorized reproduction of a particular organization of the independent bits of information contained in the entire compilation which was in some sense "originated" or "created" by the person responsible for producing the compilation. The limited nature of protection afforded to "fact" compilations by copyright gave little cause for concern on the part of proprietors of multi-volumed printed bibliographic records, which did not lend themselves to any kind of use or reuse that interfered with the proprietor's control over the economic value of the published works. This may no longer be the case. Data bases, including

---

[3] See e.g., the substantial bibliographies contained in G. Bush and R. Dreyfuss, eds. Technology and Copyright 3-118 (Lomond Books 1979) and in Keplinger, "Copyright and Information Technology", 1980 Annual Review of Information Science 24-33 (American Society for Information Science). In the absence of legislation or judicial decisions bearing directly on the ownership of computer data bases and software, the commentators have often engaged in esoteric discussions which do not necessarily provide answers to those faced with specific concerns.

the machine-readable bibliographic data bases produced by the agencies surveyed in this study, exist in computerized form which may be searched and copied via local or remote equipment. Some systems provide the facilities whereby data bases can be modified or expanded by contributors other than the agency that produced the original data and they can be exploited by end users in ways the originators of the data base might not sanction. Protection of data bases in this form present different problems for those asserting proprietary rights.

Certain distinct attributes of machine-readable bibliographic records exist that affect their susceptibility to legal control. Records may be created by national library agencies as well as by regional or local agencies that are formally or informally affiliated with the national agencies. They may be created by not-for-profit agencies and intended to facilitate the missions of those agencies, which include sharing the information as broadly as is feasible. Records in the systems contain nearly pure data. Whatever the format of the record, and however it is modified by other agencies, the contents of individual records are created according to rules and criteria established to make the specific factual information in that record accessible by application of computer retrieval techniques. At the present time, national bibliographic agencies differ substantially in their concern over unauthorized reproduction and distribution of their records; for example, a significant number do not claim copyright protection, nor are restrictive clauses in their exchange agreements universally applied.

This is not to suggest that copyright has no role in the protection of computer data bases of bibliographic records. The author of this section has argued[4] that the susceptibility to copyright of works stored in computer memory appears well established. No nation of which this author is aware would preclude copyright protection from a work of authorship solely because it is stored in computer memory in machine-readable form.[5] And, as noted above, nine

[4]Squires. "Copyright and Compilations in the Computer Era: Old Wine in New Bottles", 24 Bulletin of the Copyright Society 18 (October 1976).

[5]The copyright law in the United States, for example, as revised in 1976 and amended in 1980, clearly permits copyright protection for works that are stored in computer memory and disseminated by computer systems to users at computer terminals. Copyright Revision Act of 1976, 17 U.S.C. & 101 *et seq*. *See specifically*, 17 U.S.C. & 117, as amended.

of those agencies responding to this study's survey indicated that they already claim copyright in their bibliographic records. Many of the agencies responding also recognize that other agencies contribute records to their data bases and claim copyright in those records. But those who would turn to copyright as a source of protection for records in such systems---which as discussed above have significant distinct characteristics---should be aware of the very limited nature of protection afforded. They might perhaps determine that substantial reliance on copyright as a source of the control desired by national agencies or libraries over their bibliographic records in machine-readable form is misplaced and unnecessary.

The drawbacks to reliance on copyright as a basis for international protection for bibliographic records in machine-readable form which are developed, contributed to, modified, and shared internationally are many. While international conventions---primarily the Berne Convention and the Universal Copyright Convention[6]---bind virtually all the major nations currently concerned with developing and sharing bibliographic data to respect each other's copyright laws by providing reciprocal treatment, the national copyright laws themselves are not uniform. Copyright law in the United States, for example, does not permit federal government agencies to claim copyright in their publications, even though some federal agencies may express interest in obtaining such protection. While United States law is unique in this respect, the Library of Congress contains the largest collection of bibliographic records of any of the various national agencies which responded to this survey, and these records cannot be protected by copyright.

Even with regard to those nations whose copyright laws apply to works published or sponsored by public agencies, the amount of protection provided for the contents of bibliographic data systems is highly speculative. Individual

[6] Both the Berne Convention and the Universal Copyright Convention ("UCC"), to which most survey respondents are signatories (the notable exception being the United States, which is a signatory of the UCC only), appear to recognize that copyright may exist for works regardless of the medium in which the works are recorded. Significantly, these international conventions do little to create substantive copyright law with respect to what works are protectable; rather, they recognize reciprocal treatment among member nations.

bibliographic records---containing pieces of information about a certain work or author---are about as close to purely factual, and therefore uncopyrightable, works as one is likely to find. The fact that one nation's system---or an agency contributing records to it---may organize the data in its individual records in a slightly different fashion than does another, provides little, if any, additional basis for asserting copyright in the individual records of factual information. A system may be susceptible to copyright insofar as the individual records are organized systematically, and copyright may protect against the unauthorized replication of substantial segments of the records in the system because then the copyrightable element of a compilation---the organization of the records inter se---has been copied. In addition, not all national bibliographic agencies claim copyright protection for the systems of records they produce.

The concerns of the producers of bibliographic data appear to be with determining whether or not, and on what terms, access to other users should be granted, and what controls on copying, varying levels of modification, and redistribution of records acquired as a result of that access should be permitted. The concern, expressed by some agencies which modify or contribute records, about asserting proprietary rights in records as modified or contributed is really another aspect of seeking to control access and use via control over copying or redistribution of data to third parties. It is our opinion that none of these concerns are well-suited to be controlled by assertion of copyright in the machine-readable data bases produced by national bibliographic agencies, especially through reference to existing copyright laws.

In the first instance, copyright was never designed to function as a body of law to govern relationships of parties seeking to control distribution of works to a limited audience. Rather, even in the early days of printing, copyright was a tool to control unauthorized distribution of works intended for broad dissemination that would immediately be beyond the control of a work's publisher. Copyright was necessary to control dissemination of works of authorship because agreements among parties were not sufficient.

Most issues concerning reuse of information acquired by searching one agency's bibliographic records cannot be satisfactorily resolved by sole reliance on copyright law. It would be possible, for example, for the authorized searcher of such records to "repackage" or "resell" the information obtained from a search to yet another. But the actual practices of the bibliographic record users studied here (i.e., national bibliographic agencies) do not seem to be of a sort that would constitute copyright violations, because they do not reproduce and re-exploit copyrightable elements of the MARC data bases. (This may change, however, with increasing use of on-line systems and satellite transmission across national boundaries.)

It is apparently common practice, as revealed by the survey results, for national bibliographic agencies to modify the individual records they receive from other agencies---either by deleting portions, adding information, or restructuring the data in the record. Such "reformatting" of individual records is probably not a copyright violation, nor does it give the agency a copyright interest in the record as modified. Copyright provides no protection for individual records contained within bibliographic data collections, and the "format" of such individual records, which are presumably arranged solely to present the information in a useful manner---is not truly a copyrightable element of a fact compilation.

The survey also indicates that half the responding national agencies, including all those with highly developed systems, obtain records from other agencies, and most of those distribute these records to yet other agencies. The contributions of individual records to a comprehensive system gives the contributor no real copyright interest in the entire system. As indicated above, there is probably not any copyrightable element in an individual record. The copyrightable element in a fact compilation is the structural relationship---the systematization---of the collection of individual records. Agencies contributing individual records make no real creative contribution to the overall structure of a pre-existing system.

Finally, it does not appear that the actual "resale" by a national bibliographic agency of a large segment of contiguous records in a machine-readable bibliographic data base---the one type of unauthorized use which would most likely constitute a copyright violation because it replicates the system's organization---is the type of use about which system proprietors and users are really concerned. There is little likelihood that an authorized user (one of the national agencies which participates in the national or international sharing of records) would "bleed off" substantial components of a system and try to remarket them. However, if this were a problem, or were it to become a practice which agencies could not control by simple agreement,[7] then the existence of copyright might give a producing agency an enforceable copyright interest in its system.

Moreover, one agency's act of repackaging data obtained from such an authorized use of another's data collection may not be a copyright violation if the information is restructured for a different use. This conclusion is suggested by a recent case in the United States, in which a court held that it was not a copyright violation for a party to search the New York Times Index, a well-known reference compilation, in order to create a new directory indexing names cited in the Times Index.[8]

This is not to say that national bibliographic agencies responsible for the creation and dissemination of bibliographic records in machine-readable form, or the various contributors of data to such systems, can have no control over the information compiled in the system. It is only to say that copyright law seems not to be necessary to provide them with the control they seek.

Those who create and make contributions of value to data compilations such as MARC-type data bases do have the threshhold power to grant or withhold access to other agencies or users of the records they have compiled. The information they collect and input is proprietary in the sense that they have physical possession of the data base they have developed. According to the value their contribution has to others with whom they may wish to share those records, creators and proprietors of bibliographic compilations may bargain concerning the terms on which they will make their records available to others.

They may, for example, seek reciprocal access to the records of other systems in return for access to the records they create. They may seek to charge a user fee; whether it is called a license or royalty payment or given another name is of no consequence. Such fees might be charged based on time spent searching a particular data base or on the number of records retrieved in

[7] For example, via current exchange agreements' inclusion of a prohibition against the publication by one agency of another agency's national bibliography.
[8] New York Times Co. v. Roxbury Data Interface, Inc., 434 F. Supp. 217 (D.N.J. 1977).

any search. They may also seek to charge additional fees to any user who grants access to yet other parties, and assess some type of charge, or demand some type of service, for that access. The assertion of copyright is not necessary to make such agreements enforceable. Lawful possession of the physical medium is sufficient control to enable agencies to enter such agreements and to discontinue the relationships if they choose if the other parties refuse to comply with their responsibilities.

It is not here contended that use and access to any and all machine-stored information can be adequately limited by such arrangements, in such a way that the economic contributions of creators and proprietors can be fully protected. But it is contended that such contractual arrangements, based purely on the agreement of parties acting in good faith to set the terms on which they will deal with each other, may be appropriate to create adequate legal relationships among national agency bibliographic data base publishers, contributors and users, both now and in the foreseeable future.

Computer Software

The other element of computerized data retrieval systems that may provide some basis for control of the data provided by use of such a system is the computer program designed to direct a system's function. While great attention has been focused on ways in which the developer of a computer program may secure exclusive rights to exploit that program, relatively little attention has been given to using ownership in a program to determine rights of ownership and access with regard to information provided by a computerized data retrieval system.

Computer programs are often tailored to perform specific data manipulation procedures. Ownership of a program designed to govern these procedures gives the proprietor the power to control the systematic manipulation of data for which the program is created. And while the international community has reached no agreement as to what legal principles apply to protect computer programs,[9] ownership of a program can provide the basis for limiting access to the program, and thus access to the information stored in any retrieval system.

The legal protection on which creators of computer programs who wish to protect their proprietary rights place greatest reliance is satisfied by imposing contractual restraints on the rights of their customers to use or make available to others their software. When distribution of software products is limited to specific customers, the owner of software may properly assert that the software constitutes trade or industrial secret information, which will enable a proprietor to enforce contractual limitations on those desiring to license the software.

To the extent that proprietors of MARC-type systems can control access to the software that operates the electronic searching and retrieval of records in their data bases, they will be able to prohibit the use of their data bases. Much as in the case with control of the data base itself, the control of software, whether under claim of patent, copyright, or industrial secret protection, is most useful---to those who wish to regulate the very particular types of uses likely to be made of MARC records---as a mechanism for bargaining rights and conditions of access to the data retrieval system. And for this purpose, it is relatively insignificant whether the control of the system is based on any of the above legal categories, or simply on the basis of willingness to enter into

[9] There is wide divergence in the laws applied in different nations to protect computer programs, although there is apparently uniform agreement that the creators and proprietors of programs are entitled to protection against unauthorized use. The United States provides a kind of microcosm of the different approaches to the protection of computer programs that exist in the international community. As recently amended, United States copyright law is clearly intended to provide some protection for computer software. See Copyright Revision Act of 1976, 17 U.S.C. & 101 and 117, as amended. It is unclear, however, what the scope of protection afforded by copyright is, and whether protection extends to programs in both their object code, i.e., the machine encoding that interacts directly with a computer, and their source code, i.e., the program as actually written by a programmer in symbolic terms intended to be read and interpreted by others. At least one American court has suggested that copyright does not apply to programs in their machine-encoded form. Data Cash Systems v. J.A. & A Group, Inc., 480 F. Supp. 1063 (N.D. Ill. 1979), aff'd on other grounds, 628 F.2d 1038 (7th Cir. 1980).

sharing agreements. For the uses of MARC records which can reasonably be foreseen, contractual arrangements, irrespective of claims to intellectual property rights, should be a sufficient basis for proceeding.

Conclusion

The responses to the survey giving rise to this report indicate that a slight majority of national agencies responding assert copyright in the bibliographic records they produce. Yet the responses do not indicate that the majority of agencies responding place great reliance on current copyright laws as a source of protection. These responses may reflect accurate perceptions that technological changes have outpaced the capacity of legal protection designed for what are now "old-fashioned" modes of communication.

The agencies responding to the survey indicated that agreements among user organizations or changes in their nations' copyright laws (reflecting a perceived inadequacy of current copyright laws) are among the most desired means for creating adequate legal relationships among bibliographic data base creators and users. (Fourteen respondents indicated support for electronic controls over on-line access to bibliographic records. This is not really a legal system, but rather a technical mechanism for implementing and accounting for activity.) Relatively little support was shown for compulsory or multinational systems---whether by some form of blanket or compulsory license or international clearinghouse of rights. It is likely that this lack of support reflects the appreciation of the system proprietors that such systems are either too inflexible, or are unnecessarily burdensome, to regulate their activities.

The responses indicating a desire for changes in copyright laws reflects a desire for greater certainty and more directly applicable legal rules to govern rights in data information systems in general, and bibliographic data bases in particular. Such changes in the various nations' laws are likely to be slow in forthcoming. And any changes that are enacted will not be easily applicable to particular international sharing problems. It is the point of this essay that such changes are not necessary for the national bibliographic agencies which are proprietors and users of MARC-type systems to establish adequate legal relationships for the continuation and development of data base sharing among the national agencies surveyed.

SECTION 4
DISCUSSION OF SURVEY FINDINGS

4.1 Introduction

In the previous section we limited our legal discussion to the applicability of copyright law to governing the exchange of bibliographic data among the national bibliographic agencies. As we will see in this section, the national bibliographic agencies also distribute and receive data to and from many other agencies, especially in the countries in which the agencies are located. Also, in this section, the reader should note that "DK" in a statistical table signifies a "don't know" response, while "NR" signifies that no response was given.

4.2 Summary

Almost three-fourths of the 1.5 million machine-readable records to be added by the 21 responding agencies were accounted for by five countries: Denmark, Sweden, South Africa, the United Kingdom, and the United States. Thus, the bulk of bibliographic record production is accounted for by a relatively small number of countries, suggesting that the economic interests of countries involved in exchange may also differ substantially.

Only five countries (Singapore, Denmark, Malaysia, United States, South Africa) base at least 22% of their records to be added in 1981 at least partially on machine-readable records obtained from other organizations. Altogether, these agencies account for about half of the machine-readable records to be added in 1981, indicating, at least numerically, a high reliance upon machine-readable data for cataloging purposes.

Only nine agencies actually claim copyright protection for their machine-readable records. Eight agencies report that neither computerized data bases nor computer programs are protected by their nation's copyright laws. Only two agencies reported that their countries discourage, restrict, or control distribution of machine-readable bibliographic records across national boundaries.

We divided bibliographic data exchange into two categories: exchange between the agency and other organizations within its own country, and exchange with organizations outside its country.

Only four agencies (U.K., U.S., Denmark, South Africa) reported they received machine-readable bibliographic records from organizations within their country. The United Kingdom reported that all of the records which it received from its 48 domestic contributors were covered by copyright. The United States reported that none of the records received from its 18 domestic contributors were covered by copyright.

Eight agencies reported that they distributed machine-readable bibliographic records to organizations within their countries; the majority of the U.K.'s domestic recipients (23 out of 30) were organizations funded by local governments. About half (21 out of 43) of the United States' domestic recipients were commercial, for-profit, or private sector organizations, while 19 were networks, utilities, or academic, public, or state libraries. Only four of these eight agencies have formal exchange agreements with the domestic recipients of their records.

Six agencies report that organizations within their countries provide on-line access to their records. The United Kingdom (which claims copyright protection for its bibliographic records) is the only country whose national bibliographic agency derives income or revenue from the on-line service provided by these other domestic organizations.

We turn now to exchanges with organizations outside the national bibliographic agencies' own national boundaries. We found that ten agencies in 1980 (about half of those responding) received machine-readable bibliographic records from organizations outside their own country; these ten agencies include Canada, U.S., Denmark, France, South Africa, U.K., Japan, Malaysia, Singapore and Thailand. At least eight of these ten agencies receive bibliographic records from at least one foreign organization which claims copyright protection for its bibliographic records.

Seven responding agencies (U.S., Thailand, Philippines, U.K., France, Denmark, Canada) distribute records in machine-readable form to organizations outside their country. At least three of these countries (Canada, U.K., U.S.) report that these foreign exchange partners provide on-line access to their records. None report deriving any money from participation in such arrangements. Ten agencies report they have formal exchange agreements with foreign organizations. Six agencies report having exchange agreements which cover both the receipt as well as distribution of data (France, U.S., Denmark, Thailand, U.K., Canada). Five have agreements which cover only the distribution of data (France, U.S., Thailand, U.K., Canada). Seven have agreements which cover only the receipt of data (Denmark, Thailand, Sweden, South Africa, Singapore, Malaysia, Canada). (Due to the large number of agreements which cover both distribution and receipt, it is not possible to estimate how many unique exchange partners and/or exchange agreements exist, since several countries may distribute and receive records with the same foreign organization.)

Of the total of 21 responding agencies, eleven provide computerized on-line access to their bibliographic records. Only four of these eleven agencies report that they provided on-line access to individuals or organizations outside their country. Only two of the eleven derive any income from this service.

When asked how the machine-readable bibliographic records they obtained from other organizations were used, three uses were mentioned most frequently: searching, examining, or viewing individual records or data elements without copying, modifying, or duplicating them; changing or altering the contents of one or more of the data elements in the bibliographic record; and, preparing a paper or microform copy of the machine-readable bibliographic records. Least frequently mentioned was the making of exact copies.

When asked more specifically to identify the type of application made of the information obtained from the machine-readable bibliographic records, two applications were mentioned most frequently: used to search for cataloging data; and, used to help produce a data base which is available for on-line searching or examination.

Respondents were also asked to rank a variety of "control mechanisms" which were possibly relevant to controlling the international exchange of bibliographic records. The following mechanisms received the strongest support: changes in national copyright laws; bilateral exchange agreements; and, electronic means of controlling distribution.

Finally, agencies were asked to indicate how often eight specific components were included in the formal exchange agreements they had entered into with organizations to which they currently supply machine-readable bibliographic records. Currently, the component which occurs most frequently in such exchange agreements is that records must be provided in MARC/UNIMARC format. Agencies also indicated the exchange agreement components which they intend to include in the future. The two components most frequently mentioned were (1) the receiving organization agrees not to produce a competing product or service, and (2) the receiving organization may not copyright a product or service based on the supplied machine-readable bibliographic records.

4.3 Discussion

The picture which these data provide is one of a complex international exchange system, governed by both formal and informal exchange agreements, in which producing agencies are increasingly concerned with questions of controlling the use and/or modification of their records. The degree to which copyright protection is sought varies substantially from country to country, even among the major producers. Few organizations derive any significant income from the sale or distribution of their records. Recipient organizations use records in not-unexpected ways, either as part of their ongoing cataloging or library services, or for inclusion in their distribution of records in paper, microform, or computerized form. Despite the wide acceptance of standardization, the degree of record modification appears to be relatively high.

We conclude that use of the machine-readable records by the national agencies can be characterized as the operation and expansion of traditional library bibliographic sharing programs, facilitated now by computer technology. Without addressing the question of economic viability, it would appear that the international exchange partnerships operate successfully.

The concern about record use and modification which was one of the driving forces behind generating this study may not be caused, we suspect, by the activities of the national agencies themselves. Instead (drawing upon our interview findings) concern about record use and modification derives from concern about the activities of third-party organizations such as networks, consortia, and commercial organizations. Agencies regularly modify (to varying degrees) the records they receive before including them in their own bibliographic systems. Contributing organizations cannot directly control how third party organizations may use their records. We thus draw the following conclusions. First, a standardized mechanism such as a universal exchange agreement is neither feasible nor desirable. Second, if agencies' concern about modification continues to increase, if demands that producing agencies share in proceeds from sale to or by third parties continues to increase, and if universal applicability and/or use of copyright continues to be an uncertainty (as we expect to be the case for the forseeable future), then restrictions may develop concerning the sharing of bibliographic data on an international basis. These restrictions may threaten the attainment of universal bibliographic control unless steps are taken to promote a balancing of the rights of producers and users.

We freely admit that this is primarily an economic interpretation of the problems which arise when computerized data are shared and uncertainties or unevenness exist regarding copyright. It does not fully take into account the "moral rights" basis for copyright which is felt more strongly by European producers, for example. Nevertheless, the economic uncertainties which have arisen may very well overshadow the moral rights considerations if producing organizations do not feel they are receiving a "fair share" of revenues generated from data they originally produced. If such concerns are not assuaged, then there may be cause for concern about the future international exchange of bibliographic data under current arrangements.

4.4 Survey Tabulations

4.4.1 Production of Bibliographic Records in Machine-Readable Form

Eighteen of the 21 responding agencies (see Table 4.1) reported they would produce bibliographic records in machine-readable form in 1981. Of the total 1.5 million machine-readable records to be added by these agencies in 1981, almost three-fourths (73%) were accounted for by only five countries: Denmark, Sweden, South Africa, United Kingdom, and the United States. These countries also account for the largest number of bibliographic records in machine-readable form at the end of 1980, with approximately 88 percent of the total seven million records.

All of the agencies report the addition of records by means of original cataloging, ranging from 581 in 1981 for Nigeria to 183,800 for the United States. Nine agacies reported that they based at least some of their added records on cataloging data obtained from other organizations. Not surprisingly, these agencies which use cataloging data obtained from other countries usually do so by means of data in machine-readable form.

In fact, several countries depend primarily on machine-readable records obtained from other organizations to serve as input to their databases. For example, of the 275,000 records Denmark expected to add during 1981, 247,000 (90%) were to be based at least partially on cataloging data obtained in machine-readable form from other organizations. Twenty-one thousand of Malaysia's 30,000 records added in 1981 were to be based at least partially on machine-readable data. Nearly all (49,000 of 50,000) of Singapore's added records were to be based on machine-readable records. South Africa and the U.S. both rely on machine-readable data with 22 percent of South Africa's and 25 percent of U.S. projected 1981 additions being based at least partially on machine-readable bibliographic records.

Table 4.2 displays a ranking of countries by the percentage of 1981 added records based at least partially on machine-readable data from other countries. The top five countries listed here (Singapore, Denmark, Malaysia, United States, South Africa) account for about half of the machine-readable

Table 4.1 Production of Bibliographic Records in Machine-Readable Form

Country	Question Number[1]					
	1	2	3	4	5	6
Austria	No	--	--	--	--	--
Bulgaria	No	--	--	--	--	--
Canada	Yes	290,000	50,000	30,000	20,000	4,000
Czechoslovakia	--	--	--	--	--	--
Denmark	Yes	2,000,000	275,000	28,000	247,000	247,000
Finland	Yes	45,000	15,000	15,000	0	0
France	Yes	130,000	25,000	25,000	0	0
Italy	Yes	72,000	72,000	72,000	0	0
Japan	Yes	147,000	50,000	50,000	0	0
Korea	Yes	4,800	8,000	8,000	0	0
Malaysia	Yes	47,000	30,000	9,000	21,000	21,000
Nigeria	Yes	1,061	617	581	36	0
Philippines	Yes	22,430	40,000	3,000	800	0
Singapore	Yes	30,167	50,000	1,000	49,000	49,000
Spain	Yes	25,000	26,000	26,000	0	0
Sweden	Yes	450,000	300,000	140,000	NR	NR
Taiwan	Yes	2,600	33,000	33,000	0	0
Thailand	Yes	2,500	4,068	2,068	2,000	0
S. Africa	Yes	600,000	135,000	12,000	123,000	30,000
United Kingdom	Yes	1,153,000	126,000[2]	126,000	0	0
United States	Yes	2,068,300	243,800	183,800	60,000	60,000

SOURCE: King Research, Inc., IFLA International Study of Copyright of Bibliographic Records in Machine-Readable Form, 1981

[1]Questions:

1. Will your agency produce any bibliographic records in machine-readable form during 1981?
2. What is the estimated number of bibliographic records your agency possessed in machine-readable form at the end of 1980?
3. How many bibliographic records in machine-readable form do you expect to add during 1981?
4. Of the total figure estimated in Question 3 above, how many of the added records will be the result of original cataloging done by your agency?
5. Of the total figure estimated in Question 3 above, how many of the added records will be based at least partially on cataloging data obtained from other organizations?
6. Of the number estimated in Question 5, how many of these added records will be based at least partially on cataloging data obtained in machine-readable form from other organizations?

[2]Refers to records produced by the British Library itself.

Table 4.2 Ranking of Agencies by the Percentage of Their 1981 Added Records Which Are Based at Least Partially on Machine-Readable Data Obtained From Other Organizations

Ranking	Percent[1]	Countries[2]
1	98%	Singapore
2	90%	Denmark
3	70%	Malaysia
4	25%	United States
5	22%	South Africa
6	8%	Canada
7	0%	Finland, France, Italy, Japan, Korea, Philippines, Spain, Taiwan, Thailand, United Kingdom[3], Nigeria

SOURCE: King Research, Inc., IFLA International Study of Copyright of Bibliographic Records in Machine-Readable Form, 1981

[1]Percent of records to be added in 1981 which are based at least partially on machine-readable records obtained from other organizations.

[2]Countries not supplying answer to question #6: Sweden.

[3]U.K. reports that, while receipt of machine-readable data does occur from organizations inside and outside that country, "...there is at present no routine acceptance of cataloging data from sources external to the British Library".

data to be added in 1981, suggesting a modest correlation between the volume of records to be added and the use of externally-supplied machine-readable data.[1] It may be premature to suggest that volume of catalog input causes a reliance on machine-readable data (as opposed to other sources) due to cost considerations, since the ability to use machine-readable input (i.e., available hardware, software, and trained staff) may itself be a motivating factor in the ability to expand one's catalog. Nevertheless, it is clear that reliance upon externally-generated machine-readable data is substantial, and that a significant number of the supplying organizations do claim copyright protection.

---

[1]These same five countries also account for 67 percent of the reported total size of machine-readable bibliographic databases at the end of 1980.

4.4.2 Copyright Status

Nine national bibliographic agencies currently claim copyright protection for their machine-readable bibliographic records. Of the countries which do not, there are none in which efforts are underway to change this. The only national bibliographic agencies indicating that there are efforts underway to "claim, extend, modify, or clarify copyright coverge" of their machine-readable bibliographic data bases are those which already claim copyright coverage.

Question 42 (Table 4.3) asks specifically about whether or not computerized data bases and/or computer programs are specifically subject to the protection provided by the country's copyright laws. The confusing aspect of the answers to this question is that a number of countries (Canada, France, Malaysia, Singapore, South Africa and the United Kingdom) report that neither data bases nor programs are specifically covered by copyright, but they claim copyright protection for their machine-readable bibliographic records. This would seem to indicate that merely claiming copyright protection does not provide a very solid basis for protecting these bibliographic records since one can assume there is not a large body of case law defining the parameters of such protection.

National bibliographic agencies reflect decisions and policies of the national governments of which they are a part. One concern addressed by this survey was whether or not national transborder dataflow policies of various countries might substantially impede the free flow of information, particularly the distribution or transmission of machine-readable bibliographic data. Only two agencies, the national bibliographic agencies of Austria and Malaysia, reported that they were subject to governmental restrictions relating to the distribution or transmission of their machine-readable bibliographic records.

Table 4.3 Copyright and Bibliographic Records in Machine-Readable Form

Countries Which Produce Machine-Readable Bibliographic Records	Question Number[1]								
	40	41	42-1	42-2	42-3	42-4	42-5	43	45
Austria	NA	No	X	X				No	Yes
Bulgaria	NA	NR						No	NR
Canada	Yes	No				X		Yes	No
Czechoslovakia	NR	NR						NR	NR
Denmark	NR	NR						NR	NR
Finland	Yes	Yes			X			Yes	No
France	Yes	Yes				X		No	No
Italy	No	No					X	DK	DK
Japan	Yes	No			X			No	No
Korea	No	No				X		No	DK
Malaysia	Yes	No				X		DK	Yes
Philippines	No	No		X				No	No
Singapore	Yes	No				X		Yes	No
Spain	Yes	DK					X	DK	No
Sweden	No	DK					X	DK	No
Taiwan	No	DK					X	DK	No
Thailand	No	No				X		No	No
South Africa	Yes	Yes				X		Yes	No
United Kingdom	Yes	Yes				X		No	No
United States	No	No						No	No

SOURCE: King Research, Inc., IFLA International Study of Copyright of Bibliographic Records in Machine-Readable Form, 1981

[1] Question:

40. Does your organization claim copyright protection for your machine-readable bibliographic records?
41. Are there efforts currently underway within your organization or elsewhere in your country to claim, extend, modify, or clarify copyright coverage of your machine-readable bibliographic records?
42. Are computerized data bases or computer programs specifically subject to the protection provided by your country's copyright law? 42-1=Databases, 42-2=Programs, 42-3=Both Databases and Programs, 42-4=Neither Databases nor Programs, 42-5=Don't Know.
43. Are efforts currently underway in your country to add to, extend, or modify your country's copyright law with respect to explicit coverage of computer programs or computer databases?
45. Does your government, through any of its laws, regulations, tariffs, or import/export restrictions discourage, prevent, restrict or otherwise control the distribution or transmission in any form of your machine-readable bibliographic records across national boundaries?

4.4.3 Exchange Within the National Bibliographic Agency's own Country

Receipt of Machine-Readable Bibliographic Records from Organizations Within National Bibliographic Agency's Own Country

Four of the responding agencies indicated that they received machine-readable bibliographic records from organizations within their own countries. The United Kingdom received records from 48 such organizations, the United States from 18, and Denmark and South Africa 9 and 4 respectively (see Table 4.4).

The number of records received by each national bibliographic agency from organizations within its country varies from 95,000 for South Africa to 65,000 for the United States. The United Kingdom did not respond to this question.

The third aspect of this information is the number of these records received by the national bibliographic agency which were covered by copyright. The responses ranged from "all" for the unreported number of records for the United Kingdom to zero for the United States. South Africa reported that all but 1,000 of the records they obtained were covered by copyright, while only 12,000 of the 80,000 records obtained by Denmark were so covered. The small number of bibliographic agencies reporting on this question and the wide range of responses concerning coverage by copyright of bibliographic records in machine-readable form which they obtain from organizations within their countries make drawing broad conclusions from these data inappropriate.

Table 4.4 Receipt of Machine-Readable Bibliographic Records from Organizations Within National Bibliographic Agency's Own Country

Country	Question[1]			
	7	8	9	10
Denmark	Yes	9	80,000	12,000
South Africa	Yes	4	95,000	94,000
United Kingdom	Yes	48	NR	"All"
United States	Yes	18	65,000	0

SOURCE: King Research, Inc., IFLA International Study of Copyright of Bibliographic Records in Machine-Readable Form, 1981

[1] Questions:

7. Did your agency receive any bibliographic records in machine-readable form during 1980 from other organizations located within your country?
8. From how many other organizations located within your country did you receive machine-readable bibliographic records during 1980?
9. What was the total number of bibliographic records in machine-readable form which you received in 1980 from other organizations located in your country?
10. Approximately how many of the bibliographic records reported in Question 9 were covered by copyright?

Distribution of Bibliographic Records in Machine-Readable Form to Organizations Located Within the National Bibliographic Agency's Own Country

Eight national bibliographic agencies reported distributing their machine-readable bibliographic records to organizations within their own country. The United States distributed records to the most organizations as Table 4.5 shows. Of the 43 organizations receiving the United States records, 21 were private-sector organizations, 19 were networks, utilities, or academic, public, and state libraries.

The United Kingdom distributed its records to thirty organizations within the U.K., by far the majority of which (23) were to organizations funded by local government. Canadian national bibliographic records were distributed by the National Library of Canada to 23 organizations within Canada, 17 of which were libraries and educational institutions. The remaining national bibliographic agencies distributed their records to significantly fewer organizations within their own countries. South Africa provided records to four organizations, Italy to three, and Sweden, Thailand, and Finland to one each.

It is clear that most of this kind of distribution of machine-readable bibliographic records is being done by the United States, the United Kingdom, and Canada, with most of their records going to libraries and library networks. Only the United States has a sizable distribution to commercial or private sector organizations.

Table 4.5 Distribution of Bibliographic Records in Machine-Readable Form to Organizations Located Within the National Bibliographic Agency's Own Country

Country[2]	Question Number[1]			
	19	20(a)	20(b)	20(c)
United States	43	3	21	19
Thailand	1	0	0	1
Sweden	1	0	1	0
Italy	3	2	0	1
United Kingdom	30	3	3	24
South Africa	4	4	0	0
Finland	1	1	0	0
Canada	23	3	3	17

SOURCE: King Research, Inc., IFLA International Study of Copyright of Bibliographic Records in Machine-Readable Form, 1981

[1]Questions:

19. To how many organizations within your country did you distribute these bibliographic records?
20. How many of the organizations in your country to which you distributed your bibliographic records in machine-readable form were:
    a) Operated by or receive the majority of their funds from your national government?
    b) Commercial, for-profit, or private-sector organizations?
    c) Other (please describe)

[2]Only those countries which responded "yes" to question #18 are tabulated here. Question #18 read: Did your agency distribute any bibliographic records in machine-readable form (for example, on computer tape, punched cards, or other storage media) during 1980 to other organizations located within your country?

Other Organizations Within the National Bibliographic Agency's Own Country Which Provide On-Line Access to Its Records

On-line access to the national bibliographic records of six countries is provided by other organizations within those countries, according to the results of our survey. As Table 4.6 shows, eighteen organizations provide access to the bibliographic records of the United States, eight to Canadian bibliographic records, three to the records of Italy and the United Kingdom. Only the United States has commercial, for profit, or private sector organizations providing on-line access to its bibliographic records and, interestingly, derives no revenue from this service. The United Kingdom is the only country whose national bibliographic agency derives income or revenue from the on-line service provided by these other organizations.

Table 4.6 Other Organizations Within the National Bibliographic Agency's Own Country Which Provide On-Line Access to Its Records

Country[2]	Question Number[1]			
	30(a)	30(b)	30(c)	31
Canada	1	0	7	No
Philippines	1	0	0	No
South Africa	1	0	0	No
United Kingdom	0	0	3	Yes
Italy	2	0	1	No
United States	1	6	11	No

SOURCE: King Research, Inc., IFLA International Study of Copyright of Bibliographic Records in Machine-Readable Form, 1981

[1]Question:

30. Please estimate how many of these other organizations within your country provide computerized on-line access to the bibliographic records produced by your agency:
    a) Organizations operated by or receiving the majority of their funds from your national government
    b) Commercial, for-profit, or private-sector organizations
    c) Other (please describe)
31. Does your agency or its parent organization currently derive any money, income, or revenue from the on-line service provided by these other organizations within your country?

[2]Only countries which responded "yes" to question #29 are tabulated here. Question #29 read: At the present time do any other organizations within your country provide computerized on-line access to the bibliographic records produced by your agency?

Exchange Agreements Inside Agency's Own Country Covering Bibliographic Records in Machine-Readable Form

Only four national bibliographic agencies (see Table 4.7) reported having formal exchange agreements with other organizations within their own countries. Of these agencies, South Africa had the greatest number (six), followed by the United States and Italy with three each. Denmark reported one such agreement.

Table 4.7 Exchange Agreements Inside Agency's Own Country Covering Bibliographic Records in Machine-Readable Form

Country[2]	Question Number[1]			
	36(a)	36(b)	36(c)	36(d)
United States	0	0	3	3
Denmark	0	1	0	1
Italy	3	0	0	3
South Africa	2	4	0	6

SOURCE: King Research, Inc., IFLA International Study of Copyright of Bibliographic Records in Machine-Readable Form, 1981

[1]Question:

36. Please subdivide into the following categories the total number of organizations in your country with which you have formal exchange agreements:
    a) Number of organizations in your country to which you only distribute bibliographic data in machine-readable form
    b) Number of organizations in your country from which you only receive bibliographic data in machine-readable form
    c) Number of organizations in your country with which you both distribute and receive bibliographic data in machine-readable form
    d) Total (a+b+c)

[2]Only countries which responded "yes" to question #35 are tabulated here. Question #35 read: Does your agency currently have any formal exchange agreements with other organizations inside your country?

4.4.4 Exchange Outside the National Bibliographic Agency's Own Country

Receipt of Bibliographic Records in Machine-Readable Form from Outside the National Bibliographic Agency's Own Country

Ten of the agencies report that they received bibliographic records in machine-readable form in 1980 from organizations outside their country (Table 4.8). Canada and the United States each received machine-readable data from five such organizations, Denmark from four, France, South Africa, and the United Kingdom from two, and Japan, Malaysia, Singapore, and Thailand from one.

Except for Japan, and possibly Denmark, all of these agencies obtained records from agencies outside their country which claimed copyright protection for their bibliographic records. For example, more than half of the 93,300 records obtained by the United States agency from other countries were provided by agencies which claimed copyright protection. All of the 30,000 records obtained by Singapore were from organizations which claimed copyright protection. On the other hand, none of the over 200,000 records obtained by Japan were covered by copyright. Nonetheless, it is clear from Table 4.8 that most countries which obtain records from other countries obtain a "mix" of copyright and noncopyright records, suggesting that a variety of exchange agreements may be in force.

Table 4.8 Receipt of Bibliographic Records in Machine-Readable Form

Country	Question Number[1]				
	11	12	13	14	15
Austria	No	NA	NA	NA	NA
Bulgaria	No	NA	NA	NA	NA
Canada	Yes	5	1	505,569	50,794
Czechoslovakia	--	--	--	--	--
Denmark	Yes	4	NR	263,000	NR
Finland	No	NA	NA	NA	NA
France	Yes	2	2	NR	NR
Italy	No	NA	NA	NA	NA
Japan	Yes	1	0	215,025	0
Korea	No	NA	NA	NA	NA
Malaysia	Yes	1	1	200,000	200,000
Nigeria	No	NA	NA	NA	NA
Philippines	No	NA	NA	NA	NA
Singapore	Yes	1	1	30,000	30,000
Spain	No	NA	NA	NA	NA
Sweden	No	NA	NA	NA	NA
Taiwan	No	NA	NA	NA	NA
Thailand	Yes	1	1	1,193	1,193
S. Africa	Yes	2	1	184,789	45,092
United Kingdom	Yes	2	1	143,000	19,000
United States	Yes	5	3	93,300	56,000

SOURCE: King Research, Inc., IFLA International Study of Copyright of Bibliographic Records in Machine-Readable Form, 1981

---

[1] Questions:

11. Did your agency receive any bibliographic records in machine-readable form during 1980 from other organizations located outside your country?
12. From how many other organizations located outside your country did you receive machine-readable bibliographic records during 1980?
13. How many of these organizations located outside your country claimed copyright protection for the machine-readable bibliographic records which they supplied to you?
14. What was the total number of bibliographic records in machine-readable form which you received in 1980 from other organizations located outside your country?
15. Approximately how many of the bibliographic records reported in Question 14 were covered by copyright?

Distribution of Bibliographic Records in Machine-Readable Form to Organizations Located Outside the National Bibliographic Agency's Own Country

Seven of the responding national bibliographic agencies indicated that they distributed machine-readable bibliographic records to agencies outside their own countries. In most cases, the receiving agencies were those which were "operated by or received the majority of their funds from their national governments."

As can be seen in Table 4.9 the two national bibliographic agencies with the greatest distribution of such records to organizations outside their country are the United States with 19 and the United Kingdom with 18. For both of these national bibliographic agencies, as well as for Canada which placed third with 5, the majority of the organizations to which machine-readable bibliographic records were distributed were those primarily funded by their national governments. For the United States, 13 of 19 were such organizations, for the United Kingdom, 14 of 18, and for Canada, 4 of 5.

Of the total of 48 organizations which received bibliographic data in machine-readable form from the responding national bibliographic agencies, 36 or 75% were operated or received the majority of their funds from their national governments. Only 4 organizations or 8% were commercial, for-profit, or private sector organizations. The remaining nine recipients were organizations such as networks and universities.

These data would seem to indicate that most of the international exchange of bibliographic data in machine-readable form is going on between national agencies, probably national libraries or national bibliographic agencies. There is, at present, very little international exchange involving data flow between national bibliographic agencies and commercial, for-profit, or private-sector organizations.

Table 4.9 Distribution of Bibliographic Records in Machine-Readable Form to Organizations Located Outside the National Bibliographic Agency's Own Country

Country[2]	Question Number[1]			
	23	24(a)	24(b)	24(c)
United States	19	13	1	5
Thailand	1	0	0	1
Philippines	1	1	0	1
United Kingdom	18	14	3	1
France	3	3	0	0
Denmark	1	1	0	0
Canada	5	4	0	1

SOURCE: King Research, Inc., IFLA International Study of Copyright of Bibliographic Records in Machine-Readable Form, 1981

[1]Questions:

23. To how many organizations outside your country did you distribute these bibliographic records?
24. How many of the organizations outside your country to which you distributed your bibliographic records in machine-readable form were:
    a) Operated by or received the majority of their funds from their national government?
    b) Commercial, for-profit, or private-sector organizations?
    c) Other (please describe)

[2]Only countries which responded "yes" to question #22 are tabulated here. Question #22 read: Did your agency distribute any bibliographic records in machine-readable form during 1980 to other organizations located outside your country?

Other Organizations Outside the National Bibliographic Agency's Own Country Which Provide On-Line Access to Its Records

Table 4.10 indicates that very little on-line access is provided to bibliographic data by organizations outside the country whose national bibliographic agency produces the records originally. It can be definitely said that the records of only three national bibliographic agencies are made available in this manner, and only through a total of eight organizations. No national bibliographic agency reported deriving any money from participation in such an arrangement.

Table 4.10 Other Organizations Outside the National Bibliographic Agency's Own Country Which Provide On-Line Access to Its Records

Country[2]	Question Number[1]			
	33(a)	33(b)	33(c)	34
Canada	1	0	3	No
France	(See note below)			No
United Kingdom	0	0	1	NR
United States	3	DK	0	No

SOURCE: King Research, Inc., IFLA International Study of Copyright of Bibliographic Records in Machine-Readable Form, 1981

[1] Question:

33. Please estimate how many of these other organizations outside your country provide computerized on-line access to the bibliographic records produced by your agency:
    a) Organizations operated by or receiving the majority of their funds from their national government
    b) Commercial, for-profit, or private-sector organizations
    c) Other (please describe)
34. Does your agency or its parent organization currently derive any money, income, or revenue from the on-line service provided by these other organizations outside your country?

[2] Only countries which responded "yes" to question #32 are tabulated here. Question #32 read: At the present time do any other organizations outside your country provide computerized on-line access to the bibliographic records produced by your agency?

NOTE re France: "It appears that one of (the exchange agencies) has made our records accessible after conversion into their internal format, which probably cuts off online access by other libraries." (translation)

Exchange Agreements Outside Agency's Own Country Covering Bibliographic Records in Machine-Readable Form

More national bibliographic agencies reported working with more exchange agreements internationally than with organizations within their own countries, as shown in Table 4.11. Ten nations reported a total of 38 formal exchange agreements with organizations outside their own countries. The United Kingdom had a total of eleven such agreements, the majority of which were with organizations to which they distributed data. The United States and Canada each had six such agreements. Overall, most of the agreements (15 of 38) were between national bibliographic agencies and organizations with which they both distributed and received bibliographic records.

Table 4.11 Exchange Agreements Outside Agency's Own Country Covering Bibliographic Records in Machine-Readable Form

Country[2]	Question Number[1]			
	38(a)	38(b)	38(c)	38(d)
France	1	0	2	3
United States	1	0	5	6
Denmark	0	3	1	4
Thailand	1	1	1	3
Sweden	0	1	0	1
United Kingdom	9	0	2	11
South Africa	0	2	0	2
Singapore	0	1	0	1
Malaysia	0	1	0	1
Canada	1	1	4	6

SOURCE: King Research, Inc., IFLA International Study of Copyright of Bibliographic Records in Machine-Readable Form, 1981

[1] Question:

38. Please subdivide into the following categories the number of organizations outside your country with which you have formal exchange agreements:
    a) Number of organizations outside your country to which you only distribute bibliographic data in machine-readable form
    b) Number of organizations outside your country from which you only receive bibliographic data in machine-readable form
    c) Number of organizations outside your country with which you both distribute and receive bibliographic data in machine-readable form
    d) Total (a+b+c)

[2] Only countries which responded "yes" to question #37 are tabulated here. Question #37 read: Does your agency currently have any formal exchange agreements with other organizations outside your country?

4.4.5 Characteristics of Exchange Agreements

In this section we compare countries with respect to whether or not they have formal exchange agreements with the countries to which they supply bibliographic data. Then, we describe the various components of their exchange agreements.

In Table 4.12 we see that national bibliographic agencies, overall, are more likely to distribute machine-readable bibliographic data to organizations within their country than organizations outside their country. Of the 155 transfers of data tabulated in Table 4.12 only 49 involve organizations outside the supplying agency's own country. (This 49 is actually an overestimate of the number of organizations which receive data since some agencies receive data from more than one country.)

Of these 155 total transfers of data, only 36 are governed by formal exchange agreements. However, we see from Table 4.12 that exchange agreements are much more likely to be involved when records are supplied to foreign organizations; 28 of the 36 transfers governed by formal exchange agreements involve recipient organizations outside the supplying agency's own country.

We do not know why formal exchange agreements are more likely to exist with foreign than domestic organizations. The reason may be very simple: domestic organizations' use of bibliographic records may be easier to monitor, records may be distributed because of legal or regulatory requirements, or distribution may take place based on long-standing informal agreements. Alternately, formal exchange agreements may be more likely to exist for foreign distribution because of greater concerns with international standards and/or "competition." While the reasons for such differences between domestic and foreign distribution are not known from the survey, we did ask respondents to describe the characteristics of exchange agreements.

The characteristics of the exchange agreements described in Table 4.13 reflect data about those agreements pertaining to use and modification of records which the national bibliographic agencies have with organizations to whom they supply bibliographic records in machine-readable form. The most frequently occurring provision is that the originating agency must supply the

Table 4.12 Formal Exchange Agreements with Organizations Inside and Outside the Distributing Agency's Own Country

	Number of Organizations to which Data are distributed			Number of Recipient Organizations with which Agency has Exchange Agreements		
Country	Inside Country	Outside Country	Total	Inside Country	Outside Country	Total
Canada*	23	5	28	0	5	5
Denmark	0	1	1	0	1	1
Finland*	1	0	1	0	0	0
France*	0	3	3	0	3	3
Italy	3	0	3	3	0	3
Philippines	0	1	1	0	0	0
Sweden	1	0	1	0	0	0
Thailand	1	1**	2	0	2**	2
South Africa*	4	0	4	2	0	2
United Kingdom*	30	18	48	0	11	11
United States	43	19	62	3	6	9
Total	106	49	155	8	28	36

SOURCE: King Research, Inc., IFLA International Study of Copyright of Bibliographic Records in Machine-Readable Form, 1981.

*Single asterisk denotes a country which claims copyright protection in the records it produces.
**The reason for the inconsistency between these two reported numbers is unknown.

records in MARC/UNIMARC format. This component was reported by six national bibliographic agencies. Four agencies' agreements stipulated that their records may not be sold or distributed outside the receiving organization's national boundaries.

One interesting finding of this report is that while at present only one agency prohibited the production of the national bibliography or other product or service which would compete with one already being provided by that agency, eleven of the sixteen respondents indicated that such a provision would be included in the future.

The other components most agencies indicated would be included in such agreements in the future also seemed to reflect an increased tendency to protect their products. For example, the second most frequently mentioned component which would be included in the future was h which would prohibit a receiving organization from copyrighting a product or service based on the producing agency's machine-readable bibliographic records. Seven agencies indicated an intent to require receiving organizations to share use or distribution charges, although no agencies presently have such a requirement.

Whether this trend toward more focus on protecting the producing agency's product is a reflection of economic pressures being brought to bear on them, or of an increasing awareness of the value of bibliographic records in machine-readable form cannot be determined from our data. While we lean towards these interpretations, we feel that a further investigation of the rationale behind these trends should be a priority item for further research.

Table 4.13 Characteristics of Exchange Agreements

Component of Agreement	Number of Agencies Responding[1]	
	Currently appears in an agreement	Does not currently appear but will be included in the future
a) You must provide records in MARC/UNIMARC format	6	6
b) Receiving organization may not redistribute via any physical medium or channel your records in their original or modified form	1	2
c) A charge may not be imposed by the receiving organization for distribution of or access to the records	3	4
d) Any use or distribution charges imposed by the receiving organization must be shared with your organization	0	7
e) Your records may not be sold or distributed outside the receiving organization's national boundaries	4	5
f) Profit-making organizations are excluded from access to your records	2	3
g) The receiving organization agrees not to produce a national bibliography or other product or service which would compete with one already being provided by your organization	1	11
h) The receiving organization may not copyright a product or service based on your machine-readable bibliographic records	1	9

SOURCE: King Research, Inc., IFLA International Study of Copyright of Bibliographic Records in Machine-Readable Form, 1981

[1] The following countries responded to question #39: Korea, Italy, United Kingdom, Spain, South Africa, Singapore, Japan, United States, France, Taiwan, Canada, Philippines, Austria, Bulgaria, Finland, Denmark.

Question #39 was worded as follows: Listed below are some of the components or clauses which may appear in the formal agreements you have with other organizations which govern their use or modification of the machine-readable bibliographic records which you supply.

4.4.6 Computerized On-Line Access

Of the twenty-one agencies responding eleven (Table 4.14) indicated that they provide computerized on-line access to the bibliographic records which they produce. Three categories of potential users of such on-line access were identified for these records. All eleven agencies reported that their own employees or those of their parent organizations had access to on-line bibliographic records. Seven agencies reported that other individuals or organizations inside their country had on-line access to bibliographic records. Only four reported that individuals or organizations outside the country had such access.

A significant finding of this survey is that only two of the eleven agencies which report the provision of computerized on-line access to the bibliographic records they possess derive any income from the provision of this service. The questionnaire does not provide information as to why no charges are made for the use of such services by five of the seven agencies providing on-line access to individuals or organizations other than their own staff. Whether this will change if economic pressures are brought to bear on national bibliographic agencies remains to be seen.

Table 4.14 Computerized On-Line Access to Bibliographic Records in Machine-Readable Form

Country[2]	Question Number[1]			
	27(a)	24(b)	27(c)	28
Taiwan	X	X	X	No
Canada	X	X	0	No
France	X	0	0	No
Finland	X	X	X	No
Denmark	X	0	0	No
Japan	X	0	0	No
South Africa	X	0	0	No
Spain	X	X	0	No
United Kingdom	X	X	X	Yes
Sweden	X	X	X	Yes
United States	X	X	0	No

SOURCE: King Research, Inc., IFLA International Study of Copyright of Bibliographic Records in Machine-Readable Form, 1981

---

[1]Question:

27. Please put an "X" in each of the boxes below which corresponds to the categories of users who are qualified now to obtain on-line access to the bibliographic records stored on your agency's or your parent organization's computer:
    a) Employees of your agency or its parent organization
    b) Other individuals or organizations inside your country
    c) Other individuals or organizations outside your country
28. Does your agency or its parent organization currently derive any money, income, or revenue from this on-line service which you provide?

[2]Only countries which responded "yes" to question #26 are tabulated here. Question #26 read: At the present time does your own agency or your agency's parent organization operate a computer which provides computerized on-line access to the bibliographic records produced by your agency?

4.4.7 Types of Uses Made of Machine-Readable Bibliographic Data

As was suggested in the previous section, national bibliographic agencies use the machine-readable bibliographic data they receive from other organizations in a variety of ways. As can be seen in Table 4.15, the three most common types of use were:

a) Searching, examining or viewing individual records or data elements without copying, modifying, or duplicating them

c) Changing or altering the contents of one or more of the data elements in the bibliographic record

e) Preparing a paper or microform copy of the bibliographic records which you receive in machine-readable form

Ten of the 21 responding bibliographic agencies reported these types of use. The next most frequent type of use was "d) Changing the order of the data elements in the bibliographic record", followed by "h) Distributing paper or microform copies of these records to other organizations as part of your own publishing or distribution program". The remaining types of use in order of frequency with which they were reported were:

f) Deleting or erasing a portion of a record while leaving the rest of the record intact

g) Distributing machine-readable copies of these records to other organizations as part of your own publishing or distribution program

b) Making exact copies of the bibliographic records from one machine-readable medium to another

Table 4.15 Types of Uses Made of Machine-Readable Bibliographic Data Obtained from Other Organizations

	Type of Use Made of Machine-Readable Bibliographic Records Received From Other Organizations	Number of Agencies Reporting This Use[1]
a)	Searching, examining, or viewing individual records or data elements without copying, modifying, or duplicating them	10
b)	Making exact copies of the bibliographic records from one machine-readable medium to another (for example, copying from tape-to-tape or from tape-to-card)	5
c)	Changing or altering the contents of one or more of the data elements in the bibliographic record	10
d)	Changing the order of the data elements in the bibliographic records	9
e)	Preparing a paper or microform copy of the bibliographic records which you receive in machine-readable form	10
f)	Deleting or erasing a portion of a record while leaving the rest of the record intact	7
g)	Distributing machine-readable copies of these records to other organizations as part of your own publishing or distribution program	6
h)	Distributing paper or microform copies of these records to other organizations as part of your own publishing or distribution program	8
i)	Other uses[2]	1

SOURCE: King Research, Inc., IFLA International Study of Copyright of Bibliographic Records in Machine-Readable Form, 1981

[1]Countries reporting: Austria, Canada, Denmark, Japan, Korea, Malaysia, Philippines, Singapore, Sweden, Thailand, South Africa, United Kingdom, United States.

[2]Canada: "Using computer programs to convert content designators and coded data to conform with Canadian MARC specifications prior to distribution."

4.4.8 Types of Applications Made of Machine-Readable Bibliographic Data

National bibliographic agencies reported a number of types of applications made of the machine-readable bibliographic records which they received from other organizations as the following table shows. Of the twelve agencies reporting on this question, ten indicated that they used such records to search for cataloging data and/or to help produce a data base which is available for online searching or examination. The next most frequent type of application was the use of the records to produce catalog cards or catalog records. Seven agencies reported using the records as a selection tool to help in acquiring materials for a library collection, to help locate materials for interlibrary borrowing, and to help answer reference questions or inquiries supplied by library users. Other types of application mentioned by individual national bibliographic agencies are listed as footnote 2 of Table 4.16.

Table 4.16 Types of Applications Made of Machine-Readable Bibliographic Records Received from Other Organizations

Type of Application	Number of Agencies Reporting This Application[1]
a) Used as a selection tool to help in acquiring materials for a library collection	7
b) Used to help locate materials for interlibrary borrowing	7
c) Used to search for cataloging data	10
d) Used to produce catalog cards or catalog records	8
e) Used to help answer reference questions or inquiries supplied by library users	7
f) Used to help produce a data base which is available for on-line searching or examination	10
g) Other types of applications[2]	4

SOURCE: King Research, Inc., IFLA International Study of Copyright of Bibliographic Records in Machine-Readable Form, 1981

---

[1]Countries reporting: Austria, Canada, Denmark, Japan, Korea, Malaysia, Singapore, Sweden, Thailand, South Africa, United Kingdom, United States.

[2]Canada: "Provides MARC Record Distribution Service of foreign records converted to CAN/MARC format, both full tape service and selected record service." Korea: "The Union Catalogue of Foreign Books (in Korea) will be merged with ISBN (for each libraries holding) from MARC Base." Thailand: "Used to publish a union list of International Serials in South-East Asia; also, to publish ISDS-SEA Bulletin." South Africa: "Used to create order records-planned for SABINET."

4.4.9 Support for Hypothetical Control Mechanisms

As part of the survey of national bibliographic agencies, we created a list of hypothetical control mechanicsms which the national bibliographic agencies were asked to evaluate in terms of their relative support or opposition. Taking into account the fact that this list includes aspects of a variety of different control mechanisms, including economic and technical considerations as well as legal aspects, we felt that respondents' evaluations of such a list might provide guidance both for this study as well as for future international discussions concerning international data exchange.

We prefaced the list in the questionnaire with the following statement:

> "As electronic systems increase in sophistication and ease of use, it will become easier for large groups of international users to obtain access to bibliographic records in machine-readable form which are produced by organizations such as yours. Traditional mechanisms for controlling access to information, such as copyright, pricing, licensing mechanisms, and import/export laws, may need to change to accommodate changes in technology. This is especially true with regard to systems which provide on-line access on an international basis to a variety of data bases. For several years now, publishers of printed indexing and abstracting publications have been concerned that on-line access to their data bases may erode their print subscriptions. Some publishers of national bibliographies may also have similar concerns, expecially since they may wish or need to recover a portion of their costs for data base development or distribution."

Responses to this question are tabulated in Table 4.17. We display the number of countries which circled a number representing a range of opinions from "strong support" to "strong opposition", with the midpoint (3) representing "no opinion".*

According to respondents, the strongest support was given to the following mechanisms:

b) Limited or controlled access by means of agreements, contracts, or licenses with "user" organizations such as other national bibliographic agencies; no payment required

*Not all countries rated all the alternatives, hence the differences among the row totals in this table.

Table 4.17 Degree of Support or Opposition for Alternative Control Mechanisms

	Type of Control Mechanism	Number Which Support (rating= 1 or 2)	Number Which Oppose (rating= 4 or 5)	No Opinion (rating= 3)
a)	Changes in country's copyright law	14	0	3
b)	Agreements with "user" organizations	15	1	1
c)	Agreements with "intermediary" organizations	9	3	5
d)	Compulsory license	2	4	10
e)	Blanket license	4	1	12
f)	International licensing organization	4	3	10
g)	No control	7[1]	8[2]	2[3]
h)	Electronic control	15	1	1

SOURCE:

[1] Of these, 3 claim copyright protection, 3 do not claim copyright protection, and 1 (Denmark) did not specifically state that it claimed copyright protection, even though it is in the process of establishing bilateral exchange agreements.

[2] Of these, 6 claim copyright protection and 2 do not claim copyright protection.

[3] Neither of these agencies claim copyright protection (Korea and Italy).

h) Electronic control over the on-line access to your machine-readable bibliographic records; only users authorized by your organization would be supplied with an appropriate password or access code

a) Changes in your country's copyright law so that it directly addresses the use, modification, and distribution of copyrighted computer databases

The strongest opposition was shown for this alternative:

g) No control over use, modification, or distribution; only a minimal fee would be assessed by the supplying organization to cover the cost of reproducing and delivering a data tape.

One question which immediately comes to mind is whether these rankings might differ depending upon whether or not the agency claims copyright protection for the records which it produces. When we separated the responses into two groups, (1) those which produced bibliographic records in machine-readable form and claimed copyright protection, and (2) those which produced bibliographic records in machine-readable form but did not claim copyright protection,* we did not find a significant difference in the relative support given to the three alternatives most highly supported in the above analysis, i.e., changes in the country's copyright laws, agreements with "user" organizations, and electronic control methods. In other words, these alternatives were supported irrespective of whether the agency claimed copyright protection for its bibliographic records in machine-readable form.

One difference did appear between the copyright and non-copyright countries, however. This is in regard to alternative "G", which was stated in the questionnaire as follows:

> "No control over use, modification, or distribution; only a minimal fee would be assessed by the supplying organization to cover the cost of reproducing and delivery of a data tape."

---

*Countries which claim copyright protection: Canada, Finland, France, Japan, Malaysia, Singapore, Spain, South Africa, United Kingdom. Countries which do not claim copyright protection: Italy, Korea, Philippines, Sweden, Taiwan, Thailand, United States. Denmark's response on the question of copyright protection was not clear.

Apparently agencies which claim copyright protection are more likely to oppose this alternative (n=6) than support it (n=3), while those which do not claim such protection are approximately evenly split among support (n=3), opposition (n=2) and no opinion (n=2). We interpret this to mean that countries which claim copyright protection are more likely to oppose the concept of no control over record use or modification; still, three agencies which claim copyright protection do support the concept of no control over use or modification. One possible conclusion is that copyright is not viewed as sufficient for controlling or protecting the exchange of bibliographic records. While we personally agree with this conclusion, we feel that this conclusion cannot be supported by reliance upon this analysis alone, since more of the "non-copyright claiming" countries responded with "no opinion" when asked to rate the mechanism than did the "copyright-claiming" countries.

Based on these data, we conclude that:

1. Agencies which produce machine-readable bibliographic records tend to favor bilateral exchange agreements for governing the use of these records.

2. Producing agencies also support electronic control as well as copyright law-based control mechanisms.

3. About as many agencies support control over usage (n=7) as oppose control over usage (n=8), although it does appear that countries which claim copyright protection are more likely to oppose the concept of no control over use or modification.

SECTION 5

DISCUSSION OF INTERVIEW FINDINGS

5.1 Summary

The nineteen individuals interviewed (see Appendix D) represented a variety of library and non-library institutions. Essentially the same list of questions (see Appendix D) was presented to each respondent; in addition, each respondent was encouraged to comment on what issues he or she felt were important concerning the exchange of bibliographic data in machine-readable form. While the individuals interviewed represented primarily an American perspective, many of the comments they made were very relevant to the question of international exchange. Among their more salient comments were the following:

- The fact that computerized bibliographic systems provide mechanisms by which individual records can be changed was not viewed as a major concern; participants in shared cataloging systems were more concerned about the availability of their own input records.
- Unauthorized or "illegal" uses of bibliographic data were not seen yet as a major problem, possibly due to the relatively small market for such data. (This was not the case with regard to commercially-produced abstracting and indexing data, however.)
- None of the interview respondents felt that monitoring the use of individual bibliographic records was economically justifiable, given that the value of bibliographic systems derives from the availability of large compilations or sets of data.
- Respondents generally agreed with the applicability of copyright protection to compilations of bibliographic data. There was not general agreement, however, as to the applicability of copyright protection to individual records, partly because individual records are produced through the application of generalized or standardized rules.

- It was acknowledged that the costs of generating bibliographic data must be recovered. For some agencies, this happens by the provision of public funding to cover the agencies' operating costs, including all costs associated with original cataloging. Agencies without such subsidies must recover their costs in order to stay in business, whether they define themselves as not-for-profit or for-profit. The mechanisms for cost recovery varied with the objectives of the agencies and the products generated.

- Both for-profit and nonprofit producing agencies utilize some form of exchange agreements or contracts to govern the use or redistribution of their data. There was no general agreement, however, as to the importance of copyright law as the basis for such agreements.

- There was universal agreement that technology is the driving force behind the increasing ease with which bibliographic data can be exchanged. Most respondents also agreed that copyright law (and other legal mechanisms for governing exchange agreements) would lag behind technology.

- Based on these interviews, it is our conclusion that individuals who are closely familiar with the exchange of bibliographic data in machine-readable form perceive copyright as only one of the many issues with which parties to exchange must deal. It appears that more general questions such as national objectives, technology, and economics must also be dealt with, for example, in terms of the relationships between for-profit and nonprofit institutions.

5.2 Discussion of Interview Findings

One of the issues frequently mentioned as a problem area in discussions of the sharing of bibliographic data is the relationship of record ownership to record modification. This issue was addressed in the interviews. Does claiming ownership give the owner the right to prohibit record modification by users? At what point are modifications significant enough to call the modified record a new record and therefore to allow the modifying agency the right to claim ownership, and, who cares about this issue and why?

Little concern was voiced by interview respondents over the issue of changes which might be made in bibliographic records by users of a bibliographic data base. Participants in cooperative data bases stressed the need to have their original records remain unmodified in the master file to insure their usefulness to the contributing library. At least one for-profit data base representative expressed a similar point of view. As long as the fee for using the record was paid, changes in the record were not of concern to the originating company.

Many bibliographic data bases have contractual agreements with their users prohibiting sale of data from the data base to third parties. The issue of how much modification of the record makes the new modified product the possession of the modifier and seems not to have been settled definitively. Adding value to an existing record through reformatting or adding or modifying its content appears to make it subject to copyright by the agency adding the value under United States law. An example of such a case is the private press retrospective conversion of Library of Congress pre MARC catalog records into MARC format. Their product is covered by copyright, even though the source catalog records are not.

Economic Considerations

The costs of developing and distributing bibliographic records are borne by the agency or agencies doing that work. Either these costs must be covered by a subsidy of some kind, such as tax support, or they must be recovered by charging fees. In either case, the producing and distributing agency or agencies must receive returns on its investment which are considered satisfactory or it cannot long remain a producer or distributor of such information. Effective exchange agreements between agencies functioning as producers or distributors are viewed as essential for staying in business. A nonprofit data base may need only to meet operating expenses and development costs, i.e., to break even, in order to feel it has received "adequate returns" on its investment.

Agencies of each of these types can and do enter into contractual agreements specifying the responsibilities of all parties in terms of the generation, use, and distribution of the products of the bibliographic data bases. Such contracts specify ways investors receive appropriate returns and users receive appropriate benefits. No single set of benefits and recovered investment costs is appropriate for all such contracts, because the objectives of the parties differ; hence, development of a standard contract is not viewed as a satisfactory solution.

One concern which surfaced in the context of this issue is who should pay for access to and use of bibliographic data bases and how. The generation of bibliographic records by some agencies is subsidized by public funds, almost always because the producing institution is at least partially supported by such funds. The argument has been made that the subsidization could be more equitably distributed by making it available to users of the data than to its generators; the actual mechanism for accomplishing this is not clear, however.

Distinctions exist between publically supported generators of bibliographic data and commercial generators of such data. Both must recover costs appropriate to their objectives, and both must provide benefits to users within the confines of arrangements which ensure that this will happen. Common arrangements are contracts or exchange agreements which cover selling, leasing, or renting access to the bibliographic data. Various fee structures are employed, each presumably reflecting the development, maintenance, and distribution costs incurred by the data base owners. No one fee structure is appropriate for all situations.

Protection of Data Bases

Bibliographic data bases are intellectual property and are therefore entitled to some form of protection. Individuals interviewed in this study were asked to share their insights and concerns about which components of such data bases should be protected, what would be the most effective point of intervention in the creation, distribution and use cycle to ensure such protection, and what the trouble points in current protection systems are.

Some interview respondents felt that individual records on bibliographic data bases should be protected. The implementation of such a policy might in practice require the payment of royalties to the contributor each time it was used. What constitutes a "use" would need to be carefully spelled out. For a data base system whose primary service was the provision of hard copy, either of individual records or of bibliographies or some other arrangement of the data, use might be easily defined. For a data base service offering extensive search options making it useful to reference librarians, individual record use might be very hard to monitor, particularly if it consisted mainly in viewing the data on a screen. Even though the display of an individual record may be monitored by machine, how the information communicated by that display is actually used and applied cannot be realistically monitored on a real-time basis. Such a record-by-record monitoring is technically feasible; however, the question remains as to whether the associated expenses of software development, computer time, and telecommunications charges would be worth the effort. If copyright law provides the "brackets" which define an intellectual creation which is then subject to contractual arrangements, as was suggested by a number of persons interviewed, the question is then whether or not a single bibliographic record can be covered by copyright. The rationale for a negative response to this question is that bibliographic records are the products of catalogers following a universally available set of rules, not unique intellectual creations.

There were no questions raised as to the copyrightability of compilations of such records, or of the software regulating access to the data bases.

According to the interviewees, the appropriate point of intervention to provide protection for bibliographic data bases, as well as the level of that protection, varies with the objective of the data base and the needs it is designed to serve. Uses made of bibliographic data bases include the provision of cataloging information and cards, title and author verification and location information for interlibrary loans, as a resource for reference service, for acquisitions and information, for subject searches, for the generation of bibliographies, and for collection analysis. (Our survey of national bibliographic agencies covered the frequency with which such uses are made.)

"Illegal" uses of bibliographic data bases seem rare, and consist primarily of users pulling off subsets of bibliographic data which they maintain as personal information systems. Under some contractual agreements, however, this would constitute misuse only if such a private file were sold to a third party. Such a use may be the subject of a restrictive clause in an exchange agreement.

Future Developments

Almost all persons interviewed commented on one or more changes which they saw as taking place within the next five to ten years which might affect the generation and/or distribution of bibliographic data in machine-readable form. Most persons felt comfortable speculating about the changes, but not about trying to forecast the direct effect of such changes on the generation or distribution of bibliographic data, particularly internationally. What follows, therefore, is a list of areas of change, each followed by brief statements describing a change foreseen by interview respondents in that area.

A. Financial Changes

- The costs of creating and maintaining conventional card catalogs is becomming increasingly burdensome and is forcing increasing automation.

- Financial and political pressures may force publically supported institutions to attempt to recover costs, such as cataloging costs, from users or other sources.

- Fewer dollars will be available for tax supported institutions, resulting in increased cooperation.

- As the world becomes more complex, there will be increased economic incentives to have more information available faster.

B. Technological Changes

- The advent of the video disc as a medium of storage may change large data bases as they now exist in terms of how they are generated, distributed, and used.

- It may become possible to get more data into machine-readable form more cheaply.

- The greater availability of personal computers will have many ramifications for information systems. More power will be given to the end users of the systems. There will be an increasing mass market for information.

- Information, including meta-information (information about information) may become less available to people or countries without the human and financial capital to participate in technologically sophisticated information systems.

- A different catalog format may be appropriate when most records are machine-readable. Presently the format which was created for manual systems has been converted to machine-readable form, but a whole new format may become more appropriate.

C. Organizational Changes

- Role of information organizers and providers may change with advent of personal computers with capability of doing much online searching presently done by libraries and other information services.

- Publishers will increase the amount of bibliographic information they generate.

- There will be an increased number of individually oriented information services.

D. Legal Changes

- These will follow technological changes.

- Concerning international bibliographic exchanges, there will be increased attention by national governments to issues of trans-border data flow. National bibliographic agencies may be subject to increased numbers of restrictions based on developing national policies.

Magnitude of the Problem

One objective of the interviews was to determine the perceptions of a wide variety of persons about how major a problem the legal protection of bibliographic data bases really is.

By and large, persons affiliated with libraries did not feel there were major problems concerning the protection of bibliographic records in machine-readable form which were not now presently well handled by a variety of contractual relationships.

Viewpoints stated by persons in other sectors of the information community expressed a variety of concerns about the significance of the problem including the following:

- It is desirable to develop mechanisms for dealing with bibliographic data protection now because the existence of such mechanisms may prove useful when full text delivery becomes viable.

- In the context of trans-border data flow issues, the international exchange of bibliographic data is a minute portion of the concern being addressed but will be affected by the decisions made regarding, for example, the international exchange of socioeconomic data.

- Nevertheless, information is becoming an increasingly valuable international commodity. All 'subset' issues are, therefore, important, including the control of bibliographic data.

APPENDIX A

STUDY OBJECTIVES

STUDY OBJECTIVES:

International Federation of Library Associations & Institutions An International Study on the Copyright of Bibliographic Records in Machine-Readable Form

A recent survey of a number of national bibliographic agencies indicated widespread support among respondents for the international exchange of bibliographic records, as unencumbered as possible by complex financial and bureaucratic entanglements.[1] The International Federation of Library Associations (IFLA) has contracted with King Research, Inc. to conduct a study which will clarify the issues involved with such exchanges and to put forth alternative solutions to some of the problems. The major concern of this study is to explore the issues involved with copyright legislation as a method of control for bibliographic records in machine-readable formats.

Two studies have been conducted recently with slightly different foci in this issue area, the A. J. Wells study prepared for the International MARC Network Study Steering Committee in 1977[2] and the Rosenthal study done for the same organization in 1978-79.[3]

The Wells study was designed to deal with bibliographic and technical problems which would be involved in the establishment of an international MARC network. The study report recommended the establishment of an international exchange policy to be agreed upon by participating national bibliographic agencies. As summarized by Henriette Avram, the significant provisions of the agreement are:[4]

---

[1] International Access to MARC Records: A Summary Report with Recommended Text for a Bilateral Agreement for the International Exchange of MARC Records. International MARC Network Study Steering Committee. (London: IFLA International Office for UBC, 1980). Unpaginated. Summary of study by Joseph A. Rosenthal.

[2] A.J. Wells. "The International MARC Network: A Study for an International Bibliographic Data Network." Prepared for the International MARC Network Study Steering Committee. January 1977.

[3] Joseph A. Rosenthal. "International Accessiblity to Catalogue Records Prepared by National Bibliographic Agencies in the MARC Network." (Berkeley, 1978).

[4] Henriette D. Avram. "The Impact of Technology on Legislation Affecting Libraries," IFLA Journal 6 (1980) 1. 11,12.

1. The exchange of bibliographic records involves no financial charge imposed by either organization;

2. Each organization may use the other's MARC records as is or may modify records as needed;

3. The originating organization which is a copyright holder agrees that any of its records which have been modified to meet national bibliographic standards of the receiving organization are not subject to copyright;

4. Records not modified to accord with national bibliographic standards of the receiving organization may be distributed within the country of receipt to not-for-profit organizations; supply of these records to profit-making organizations is permitted but is subject to contractual arrangements made between the originating organization and the profit-making organization concerned;

5. The receiving organization agrees not to produce the national bibliography of the originating organization.

The Rosenthal study grew out of a recommendation in the Wells study for an investigation of the current situation regarding the exchange of bibliographic data between national bibliographic agencies. Twenty-five such agencies were surveyed with particular respect to their copyright situations as producers of MARC records. Findings included the following:[5]

- 18 nations are using or planning to use MARC formats for machine-readable bibliographic data

- 13 national agencies indicated their records were considered legally protected by copyright

- 11 of these 13 agencies agreed to waive copyright under bilateral or standard exchange agreements

- conditions under which copyright would be waived varied.

A question was raised but not answered in the report about the relationship of record ownership to record modification. How much can a receiving agency change

[5]From summary of Rosenthal report in International Access to MARC Records.

a record (augment, delete, reformat, etc.) before it would no longer be considered still belonging to the originating agency? Another significant group of unanswered questions concerned "use" of machine-readable records. What constitutes use and how can it be effectively measured and monitored?

The present study is being conducted for the International Federation of Library Associations and Institutions under a grant from the Council on Library Resources. The primary concerns to be addressed can be grouped into two clusters of issues. The first cluster concerns the questions arising as national bibliographic agencies move to share machine-readable data among themselves. The second thrust of the study addresses the cluster of issues involved in the distribution and use of records outside the national bibliographic agencies. It is believed that the clarification of this second cluster of issues, which is the primary focus of this study, will have an effect on the kinds of bilateral agreements national bibliographic agencies will be willing to make with one another.

Much thoughtful work has already been done concerning exchanges between national bibliographic agencies. The present study will survey national bibliographic agencies which produce machine-readable tapes, identified by IFLA, to obtain information about difficulties which presently exist for them, both as originators and as receivers of bibliographic data. Their responses will help answer questions such as the following:

- What are the present legal provisions for the protection of bibliographic files?

- What restrictions are included in exchange agreements between national bibliographic agencies?

- Are fees charged in the international exchange of national bibliographic databases? To whom? How much?

Data will also be obtained from the initial survey about the availability of bibliographic records from private sector sources and the relationship of the national bibliographic agencies to these profit and not-for-profit companies. Many private sector sources make bibliographic records available online. Online access presents a different set of control problems for bibliographic records. Information obtained from the survey augmented by information which will be obtained in interviews will be used to clarify such questions as:

- What are the interests of the national bibliographic agencies in dealing with private sector vendors of bibliographic records?

- How can both public and private sector agencies receive appropriate returns on their investments?

- Are different categories of records viewed differently so far as access? copyright?

- What is the product being protected? Data elements? Individual records? Entire data base? Software?

- Does record ownership include control of record format as well as record content?

- At what point in the distribution and use cycle should intellectual ownership rights be exercised? When access is acquired to a data base or when records are actually used?

- Are different types of protection appropriate for various levels of usage?

In evaluating alternative methods for making bibliographic records widely available, it is important to understand the priorities of the parties involved. Therefore, this study will ask national bibliographic agencies as well as a select group of concerned and knowledgeable professionals, to indicate the extent of their concerns with a variety of issues so that the evaluation criteria for the alternatives will be as comprehensive as possible. Issues such as the importance of maintaining the integrity of the record, recovering development costs, and protecting national interest in transborder data flow exchanges will be considered.

The final product of this study will be a working list of alternative solutions to the problems of international bibliographic record exchange, together with an assessment of the advantages and disadvantages of each alternative.

For further information on this study, please contact either

Dr. Margareet Wijnstroom
International Federation of Library Associations and Institutions
Netherlands Congress Building
Churchillplein 10
The Hague,
Netherlands
Tel: 070-547231

King Research, Inc.
1025 Vermont Ave., N.W., #240
Washington, D.C. 20005
Attn: Dr. Dennis McDonald (202) 393-2619
or Ms. Eleanor J. Dorsey (301) 881-6766

APPENDIX B

AGENCIES PROVIDING COMPLETE OR PARTIAL RESPONSES TO THE SURVEY QUESTIONNAIRE

Dr. K. Kozelek
Statni Knihovna Ceske
Socialisticke Republiky
Klementinum 190, PRAGUE 11001 Praha 1
Czechoslovakia

Mrs. K. Kalajdzieva, Director
Cyril and Methodius National Library
Boul. Tolbuhin 11
SOFIA
Bulgaria

Dr. G. Ustrnul, Chief
Cataloguing Division
Osterreichische Nationalbibliothek
Josefplatz 1
A-1014 WIEN
Austria

Miss Hope E.A. Clement
Associate National Librarian
National Library of Canada
395 Wellington, OTTAWA
Canada KlA ON4

Mrs. A. Salomonsen
Head, Foreign Serials Department
Det Kongelige Bibliotek
Christians Brygge 8
1219 COPENHAGEN
Denmark

Dr. E. Hakli, Director
Helsinki University Library
P.O. Box 312
SF-00171 HELSINKI 17
Finland

Mlle. M-L Bossuat
Conservateur en chef
Centre bibliographique national
Bibliothèque nationale
58, rue Richelieu
75084 PARIS Cedex 02
France

Dott.ssa Angela Vinay
Direttore
Istituto Centrale per il Catalogo
Unico delle Biblioteche Italiane e
per le Informazioni Bibliografiche
Viale del Castro Pretorio
00185 R O M A
Italy

Mr. K. Okamura, Director
Division for Interlibrary Services
National Diet Library
10-1, 1-chome, Nagato-cho
Chiyoda-ku, TOKYO
Japan 100

Hyeon Kyu Seob
The Central National Library
100-177, 1-GA
Hoe-Hyeon-Dong
Jung-Gu
CPO Box 5658
SEOUL
Korea

Mr. H.T. Lim
Chief Librarian
Universiti Sains Malaysia
Penang
Malaysia

Director S.B. Aje
National Library of Nigeria
4 Wesley Street
P.M.B.12626
LAGOS
Nigeria

Dr. Serafin D. Quiason
Director, National Library of the Philippines
T.M. Kalaw Street
Ermita, MANILA, 2801
Philippines

Mrs. Hedwig Anuar
Director, National Library
Stamford Road
SINGAPORE 6
Republic of Singapore

Mr. Hans Aschenborn, Director
State Library
P.O. Box 397
PRETORIA 0001
South Africa

Vicente Sanchez Muñoz, Director
Instituto Bibliográfico Hispánico
Calle de Atocha, 106
Apartado 12.311
MADRID 12 Spain

Miss M.-L. Bachman
Bibliografiska Institutet
Kungliga Biblioteket
Box 5039, S-10241 STOCKHOLM
Sweden

Dr. Margaret Fung
National Taiwan Normal University Library
126 Ho-Ping East Road
TAIPEI
Taiwan

Mrs. Kullasap Gesmankit, Director
National Library of Thailand
Samsen Road
TA-Vasukri
BANGKOK 3,
Thailand

Mr. Peter R. Lewis, Director General
Bibliographic Services Division
The British Library
2 Sheraton Street
LONDON W1V 4BH
United Kingdom

Mrs. Henriette Avram
Director for Processing Systems,
Networks and Automation Planning
The Library of Congress
Washington, D. C. 20540

APPENDIX C

COVER LETTER AND QUESTIONNAIRE
MAILED TO NATIONAL BIBLIOGRAPHIC AGENCIES

International Federation
of Library Associations and Institutions
Fédération Internationale des
Associations de Bibliothécaires et des Bibliothèques
Internationaler Verband
der bibliothekarischen Vereine und Institutionen
Международная Федерация
Библиотечных Ассоциаций и Учреждений

Netherlands Congress Building
Churchillplein 10
The Hague,
Netherlands
Tel.: 070-547231
Telex: 31700 NECON
Bankers:
Algemene Bank Nederland NV
Accountno: 51 36 38 911

IFLA

HEADQUARTERS

Postal address:
P.O.B. 82128
2508 EC The Hague
Netherlands

date 15 April 1981
your ref.
our ref. A4.3/631/W/CH
subject Study on copyright of bibliographic records

Dear colleague,

I write to seek your cooperation with the enclosed questionnaire from King Research, Inc. (Washington, DC) which requires your action, and I ask you to ensure that it receives prompt attention.

The questionnaire is designed to gather information to serve as the basic material on which IFLA can build a further study on the copyright of bibliographic records in machine-readable form. This study is being conducted by IFLA and is made possible by a generous grant from the Council on Library Resources.

IFLA has neither the resources nor the manpower to collect and evaluate the data on which such an important study as the present one must rely. Therefore, IFLA has decided to sub-contract the study to a firm which, in the past, has proved to be fully equipped and qualified to handle the type of research needed for a study of this kind. However, King Research will never be able to do any significant work on this project without your expertise and cooperation.

After close consultation with IFLA staff and with the Chairperson of the IFLA Section on Information Technology, your institution has been selected as one of the few institutions in the world which can be relied upon to provide the data needed and to understand the significance of the questions. *Therefore, it is vitally important that you make an effort to provide answers to these questions* - and please do not postpone working on it, but keep well within the deadline for response. Your cooperation is needed to realize this project, the object of which is to obtain the information on which can be based a plan of action for ensuring that bibliographic records can be exchanged all over the world without (or with very few) formal legal barriers.

IFLA will present the outcome of the study to the appropriate international forums. They, together, can encourage an unrestricted flow of bibliographic information on the behalf of all libraries and bibliographic agencies to meet the demands of their users.

On behalf of the IFLA Executive Board I extend my warm thanks for the time and effort devoted by you to this most important project.

Sincerely yours,

Margreet Wijnstroom
Secretary General of IFLA

THE INTERNATIONAL FEDERATION OF LIBRARY ASSOCIATIONS AND INSTITUTIONS (IFLA)
INTERNATIONAL STUDY OF COPYRIGHT OF BIBLIOGRAPHIC RECORDS IN MACHINE-READABLE FORM

SURVEY QUESTIONNAIRE

THE INTERNATIONAL FEDERATION OF
LIBRARY ASSOCIATIONS AND INSTITUTIONS
(IFLA)
INTERNATIONAL STUDY OF COPYRIGHT
OF BIBLIOGRAPHIC RECORDS IN MACHINE-READABLE FORM

INTRODUCTION

This questionnaire should be filled out by organizations which are now doing (or planning to do) one or more of the following activities:

1. Organizations which are producing a national data base of bibliographic records in machine-readable form.

2. Organizations which are distributing national bibliographic records in machine-readable form to other organizations.

3. Organizations which receive national bibliographic records in machine-readable form from other organizations such as other national bibliographic agencies.

According to the records maintained by IFLA, your organization is qualified to respond to this questionnaire. Before turning the page, please examine this mailing label and supply any necessary corrections and/or additions:

THE PURPOSE OF THIS QUESTIONNAIRE

The objectives of this study are described in the brief "Study Objectives" document which accompanies this questionnaire. This questionnaire is designed to provide information to help accomplish these objectives. In particular, the purposes of this questionnaire are as follows:

1. To learn how many bibliographic records in machine-readable form are being produced and exchanged by national bibliographic agencies.

2. To obtain information about how the distribution and use of such records is controlled.

3. To learn how national bibliographic agencies view the different available methods for controlling distribution and use of bibliographic records in machine-readable form.

The major focus of this study is the use of copyright law to control the distribution and use of bibliographic records in machine-readable form. This study, which is sponsored by the International Federation of Library Associations and Institutions (IFLA) with funding provided by the Council on Library Resources, is being conducted under contract by King Research, Incorporated, a U.S. firm which specializes in research and development related to libraries, information systems and data bases, and national information policy. Immediately upon receiving this questionnaire, please send an air-mail letter acknowledging your receipt of the questionnaire to the following address:

Dr. Dennis D. McDonald
Project Director, IFLA Study
King Research, Inc.
1025 Vermont Ave., N.W.
Suite 240
Washington, D.C. 20005
UNITED STATES OF AMERICA

You should also send the questionnaire back to this address when you are finished filling it out. We have enclosed two mailing labels for you to use.

INSTRUCTIONS

This questionnaire is divided into the following sections:

SECTION 1. Production of Bibliographic Records in Machine-readable Form

SECTION 2. Receipt of Bibliographic Records in Machine-readable Form

SECTION 3. Distribution of Bibliographic Records in Machine-readable Form

SECTION 4. Computerized On-line Access to Bibliographic Records in Machine-readable Form

SECTION 5. Characteristics of Exchange Agreements Covering Bibliographic Records in Machine-readable Form

SECTION 6. Copyright and Bibliographic Records in Machine-readable Form

SECTION 7. Mechanisms for Controlling the International Distribution and Use of Bibliographic Records in Machine-readable Form.

Throughout this questionnaire, the term "bibliographic record" is defined as follows:

> A bibliographic record is a collection of bibliographic data fields treated as one logical entity that describes a specific bibliographic item. (Library of Congress, Glossary of Library Networking Terms, 1978.)

"Machine-readable form" refers to any form appropriate for computer input, processing, or output, such as tape, disk, or cards.

Individual instructions and definitions are included in each section of the questionnaire as necessary. Please answer all the sections of the questionnaire which apply to your agency. If a question requests a number which you cannot supply or estimate, please insert the words "data not available" in the space which is provided.

PLEASE COMPLETE AND RETURN THIS QUESTIONNAIRE BY AIR MAIL TO KING RESEARCH WITHIN ONE MONTH OF THE TIME YOU RECEIVE IT.

SECTION 1

PRODUCTION OF BIBLIOGRAPHIC RECORDS IN MACHINE-READABLE FORM

1. Will your agency produce any bibliographic records in machine-readable form during 1981? (PLEASE CIRCLE 1 FOR "YES" OR 2 FOR "NO" AND FOLLOW THE DIRECTIONS.)

   Yes .... 1 (CONTINUE WITH QUESTION 2)

   No .... 2 (SKIP TO SECTION 2)

2. What is the estimated number of bibliographic records your agency possessed in machine-readable form at the end of 1980? .... ________

3. How many bibliographic records in machine-readable form do you expect to add during 1981? .... ________

4. Of the total figure estimated in Question 3 above, how many of the added records will be the result of original cataloging done by your agency? .... ________

5. Of the total figure estimated in Question 3 above, how many of the added records will be based at least partially on cataloging data obtained from other organizations? .... ________

6. Of the number estimated in Question 5, how many of these added records will be based at least partially on cataloging data obtained in machine-readable form from other organizations? .... ________

SECTION 2

RECEIPT OF BIBLIOGRAPHIC RECORDS IN MACHINE-READABLE FORM

7. Did your agency receive any bibliographic records in machine-readable form during 1980 from other organizations located within your country? (CIRCLE 1 FOR "YES" OR 2 FOR "NO" AND FOLLOW THE DIRECTIONS.)

   Yes .... 1 (CONTINUE WITH QUESTION 8)

   No .... 2 (SKIP TO QUESTION 11)

8. From how many other organizations located within your country did you receive machine-readable bibliographic records during 1980? ..... ________

9. What was the total number of bibliographic records in machine-readable form which you received in 1980 from other organizations located in your country? .... ________

10. Approximately how many of the bibliographic records reported in Question 9 were covered by copyright? .... ________

11. Did your agency receive any bibliographic records in machine-readable form during 1980 from other organizations located outside your country? (CIRCLE 1 FOR "YES" OR 2 FOR "NO" AND FOLLOW THE DIRECTIONS.)

    Yes .... 1 (CONTINUE WITH QUESTION 12)

    No .... 2 (SKIP TO QUESTION 16)

12. From how many other organizations located outside your country did you receive machine-readable bibliographic records during 1980? .... ________

13. How many of these organizations located outside your country claimed copyright protection for the machine-readable bibliographic records which they supplied to you? .... ________

14. What was the total number of bibliographic records in machine-readable form which you received in 1980 from other organizations located outside your country? .... ________

15. Approximately how many of the bibliographic records reported in Question 14 were covered by copyright? .... ________

16. Please put an "X" in the box at the right to indicate if your agency ever uses in this way any of the machine-readable bibliographic records which you receive from other organizations:

Type of use made of machine-readable bibliographic records received from other organizations	Check all boxes which are applicable to your agency
a) Searching, examining, or viewing individual records or data elements without copying, modifying, or duplicating them	☐
b) Making exact copies of the bibliographic records from one machine-readable medium to another (for example, copying from tape-to-tape or from tape-to-card)	☐
c) Changing or altering the contents of one or more of the data elements in the bibliographic record	☐
d) Changing the order of the data elements in the bibliographic records	☐
e) Preparing a paper or microform copy of the bibliographic records which you receive in machine-readable form	☐
f) Deleting or erasing a portion of a record while leaving the rest of the record intact	☐
g) Distributing machine-readable copies of these records to other organizations as part of your own publishing or distribution program	☐
h) Distributing paper or microform copies of these records to other organizations as part of your own publishing or distribution program	☐
i) Other uses (please describe): ______________________________	☐

17. Please put an "X" in the box at the right to indicate if your agency ever applies in the following ways the machine-readable bibliographic records which you receive from other organizations:

Type of application made of machine-readable bibliographic records received from other organizations	Check all boxes which are applicable to your agency
a) Used as a selection tool to help in acquiring materials for a library collection	☐
b) Used to help locate materials for interlibrary borrowing	☐
c) Used to search for cataloging data	☐
d) Used to produce catalog cards or catalog records	☐
e) Used to help answer reference questions or inquiries supplied by library users	☐
f) Used to help produce a data base which is available for on-line searching or examination	☐
g) Other types of applications (please describe): ______________ ______________ ______________ ______________ ______________ ______________	☐

SECTION 3

DISTRIBUTION OF BIBLIOGRAPHIC RECORDS IN MACHINE-READABLE FORM

18. Did your agency distribute any bibliographic records in machine-readable form (for example, on computer tape, punched cards, or other storage media) during 1980 to other organizations located within your country? (CIRCLE 1 FOR "YES" OR 2 FOR "NO" AND FOLLOW THE DIRECTIONS.)

    Yes .... 1 (CONTINUE WITH QUESTION 19)

    No .... 2 (SKIP TO QUESTION 22)

19. To how many organizations within your country did you distribute these bibliographic records? .... ______

20. How many of the organizations in your country to which you distributed your bibliographic records in machine-readable form were:

    a) Operated by or receive the majority of their funds from your national government? .... ______

    b) Commercial, for-profit, or private-sector organizations? .... ______

    c) Other (please describe): ________________________________

    ____

    ____ .... ______

21. Approximately how many copies of your bibliographic records in machine-readable form did you distribute to other organizations in your country? .... ______

22. Did your agency distribute any bibliographic records in machine-readable form during 1980 to other organizations located outside your country? (CIRCLE 1 FOR "YES" OR 2 FOR "NO" AND FOLLOW THE DIRECTIONS.)

    Yes .... 1 (CONTINUE WITH QUESTION 23)

    No .... 2 (SKIP TO SECTION 4)

23. To how many organizations outside your country did you distribute these bibliographic records? .... ______

24. How many of the organizations outside your country to which you distributed your bibliographic records in machine-readable form were:

a) Operated by or received the majority of their funds from their national government? .... ________

b) Commercial, for-profit, or private-sector organizations? .... ________

c) Other (please describe): ______________________________

____

____ .... ________

25. Approximately how many copies of your bibliographic records in machine-readable form did you distribute to organizations outside your country? .... ________

SECTION 4

COMPUTERIZED ON-LINE ACCESS TO BIBLIOGRAPHIC RECORDS IN MACHINE-READABLE FORM

NOTE: By "computerized on-line access to bibliographic records in machine-readable form" is meant that bibliographic records can be searched or examined by means of a computer terminal or other electronic device which can be connected on a permanent or temporary basis to a computer which stores the bibliographic records.

26. At the present time does your own agency or your agency's parent organization operate a computer which provides computerized on-line access to the bibliographic records produced by your agency? (PLEASE CIRCLE 1 FOR "YES" OR 2 FOR "NO" AND FOLLOW THE DIRECTIONS.)

Yes .... 1 (CONTINUE WITH QUESTION 27)

No .... 2 (SKIP TO QUESTION 29)

27. Please put an "X" in each of the boxes below which corresponds to the categories of users who are qualified now to obtain on-line access to the bibliographic records stored on your agency's or your parent organization's computer:

Category of User	Check all boxes corresponding to current users
a) Employees of your agency or its parent organization	☐
b) Other individuals or organizations inside your country	☐
c) Other individuals or organizations outside your country	☐

28. Does your agency or its parent organization currently derive any money, income, or revenue from this on-line service which you provide? (PLEASE CIRCLE 1, 2, OR 3.)

Yes 1

No 2

Don't Know .. 3

29. At the present time do any <u>other organizations within your country</u> provide computerized on-line access to the bibliographic records produced by your agency? (CIRCLE 1, 2, OR 3 AND FOLLOW THE DIRECTIONS.)

Yes .... 1 (CONTINUE WITH QUESTION 30)

No .... 2 (SKIP TO QUESTION 32)

Don't Know .. 3 (SKIP TO QUESTION 32)

30. Please estimate how many of these other organizations within your country provide computerized on-line access to the bibliographic records produced by your agency:

	Number of Organizations
a) Organizations operated by or receiving the majority of their funds from your national government	________
b) Commercial, for-profit, or private-sector organizations	________
c) Other (please describe): ____________ ______________________________ ______________________________	________

31. Does your agency or its parent organization currently derive any money, income, or revenue from the on-line service provided by these other organizations within your country? (PLEASE CIRCLE 1, 2, OR 3.)

Yes 1

No 2

Don't Know .. 3

32. At the present time do any <u>other organizations outside your country</u> provide computerized on-line access to the bibliographic records produced by your agency? (CIRCLE 1, 2, OR 3 AND FOLLOW THE DIRECTIONS.)

Yes .... 1 (CONTINUE WITH QUESTION 33)

No .... 2 (SKIP TO SECTION 5)

Don't Know .. 3 (SKIP TO SECTION 5)

33. Please estimate how many of these other organizations outside your country provide computerized on-line access to the bibliographic records produced by your agency:

	Number of Organizations
a) Organizations operated by or receiving the majority of their funds from their national government	________
b) Commercial, for-profit, or private-sector organizations	________
c) Other (please describe): ______________ ______________________________ ______________________________	________

34. Does your agency or its parent organization currently derive any money, income, or revenue from the on-line service provided by these other organizations outside your country? (PLEASE CIRCLE 1, 2, OR 3.)

Yes 1

No 2

Don't Know .. 3

SECTION 5

CHARACTERISTICS OF EXCHANGE AGREEMENTS COVERING BIBLIOGRAPHIC RECORDS IN MACHINE-READABLE FORM

NOTE: The purpose of this section of the questionnaire is to obtain information on the provisions of any formal exchange agreements you may have concerning the exchange of bibliographic records in machine-readable form between your agency and other organizations located inside or outside your country. By "formal exchange agreement" we mean an agreement between two or more organizations which governs how bibliographic data in machine-readable form will be exchanged and/or used.

35. Does your agency currently have any formal exchange agreements with other organizations inside your country? (CIRCLE 1, 2, OR 3 AND FOLLOW THE DIRECTIONS.)

Yes .... 1 (CONTINUE WITH QUESTION 36)

No .... 2 (SKIP TO QUESTION 37)

Don't Know .. 3 (SKIP TO QUESTION 37)

36. Please subdivide into the following categories the total number of organizations in your country with which you have formal exchange agreements:

	Number of Organizations
a) Number of organizations in your country to which you only distribute bibliographic data in machine-readable form	________
b) Number of organizations in your country from which you only receive bibliographic data in machine-readable form	________
c) Number of organizations in your country with which you both distribute and receive bibliographic data in machine-readable form	________
d) Total (a+b+c)	________

37. Does your agency currently have any formal exchange agreements with other organizations outside your country? (CIRCLE 1, 2, OR 3 AND FOLLOW THE DIRECTIONS.)

Yes	1	(CONTINUE WITH QUESTION 38)
No	2	(SKIP TO QUESTION 39)
Don't Know ..	3	(SKIP TO QUESTION 39)

38. Please subdivide into the following categories the number of organizations outside your country with which you have formal exchange agreements:

	Number of Organizations
a) Number of organizations outside your country to which you only distribute bibliographic data in machine-readable form	________
b) Number of organizations outside your country from which you only receive bibliographic data in machine-readable form	________
c) Number of organizations outside your country with which you both distribute and receive bibliographic data in machine-readable form	________
d) Total (a+b+c)	________

39. Listed below are some of the components or clauses which may appear in the formal agreements you have with other organizations which govern <u>their use or modification</u> of the machine-readable bibliographic records which <u>you supply</u>. For each of these components, please circle 1 or 2 to indicate if (1) this component or clause is currently included in an existing agreement, <u>or</u> (2) this component or clause does not currently appear in an existing exchange agreement but will probably be included in future exchange agreements.

Component of Agreement	Currently appears in an agreement	Does not currently appear but will be included in the future
a) You must provide records in MARC/UNIMARC format	1	2
b) Receiving organization may not redistribute via any physical medium or channel your records in their original or modified form	1	2
c) A charge may not be imposed by the receiving organization for distribution of or access to the records	1	2
d) Any use or distribution charges imposed by the receiving organization must be shared with your organization	1	2
e) Your records may not be sold or distributed outside the receiving organization's national boundaries	1	2
f) Profit-making organizations are excluded from access to your records	1	2
g) The receiving organization agrees not to produce a national bibliography or other product or service which would compete with one already being provided by your organization	1	2
h) The receiving organization may not copyright a product or service based on your machine-readable bibliographic records	1	2

NOTE: Please use the space on the following page to discuss any existing or future components of exchange agreements which are not included in the above list.

Discussion of exchange agreement components which do not appear in the list in question 39:

SECTION 6

COPYRIGHT AND BIBLIOGRAPHIC RECORDS
IN MACHINE-READABLE FORM

40. Does your organization claim copyright protection for your machine-readable bibliographic records? (CIRCLE 1 FOR "YES" OR 2 FOR "NO".)

Yes 1

No 2

41. Are there efforts currently underway within your organization or elsewhere in your country to claim, extend, modify, or clarify copyright coverage of your machine-readable bibliographic records? (PLEASE CIRCLE 1, 2, OR 3.)

Yes 1

No 2

Don't Know 3

If "yes," please explain the nature of these efforts or supply the name and address of an individual or organization who can supply additional information on this question:

____

____

____

____

____

____

____

____

____

42. Are computerized data bases or computer programs specifically subject to the protection provided by your country's copyright laws? (PLEASE CIRCLE 1, 2, 3, 4, OR 5.)

Data bases 1

Programs 2

Both of the above 3

Neither of the above 4

Don't Know 5

43. Are efforts currently underway in your country to add to, extend, or modify your country's <u>copyright law</u> with respect to explicit coverage of computer programs or computer databases? (PLEASE CIRCLE 1, 2, OR 3.)

Yes 1

No 2

Don't Know 3

If "yes," please describe these efforts or supply the name and address of an individual or organization who can supply additional information on this question:

____

____

____

____

____

____

____

____

____

44. In your view, what are the stumbling blocks, if any, to extending or clarifying copyright protection with respect to your bibliographic records in machine-readable form? Please explain, using extra sheets if necessary:

____

____

____

____

____

____

____

____

____

45. Does your government, through any of its laws, regulations, tariffs, or import/export restrictions, discourage, prevent, restrict or otherwise control the distribution or transmission in any form of your machine-readable bibliographic records across any national boundaries? (PLEASE CIRCLE 1, 2, OR 3.)

Yes 1

No 2

Don't Know 3

If "yes," please describe: ______________________________

____

____

____

____

____

SECTION 7

MECHANISMS FOR CONTROLLING THE INTERNATIONAL DISTRIBUTION AND USE OF BIBLIOGRAPHIC RECORDS IN MACHINE-READABLE FORM

As electronic systems increase in sophistication and ease of use, it will become easier for large groups of international users to obtain access to bibliographic records in machine-readable form which are produced by organizations such as yours. Traditional mechanisms for controlling access to information, such as copyright, pricing, licensing mechanisms, and import/export laws, may need to change to accommodate changes in technology. This is especially true with regard to systems which provide on-line access on an international basis to a variety of data bases. For several years now, publishers of printed indexing and abstracting publications have been concerned that on-line access to their data bases may erode their print subscriptions. Some publishers of national bibliographies may also have similar concerns, especially since they may wish or need to recover a portion of their costs for data base development or distribution.

46. On the next page we have listed a variety of "control mechanisms" which might be proposed for controlling the international modification, distribution and use of bibliographic records in machine-readable form. Some of these mechanisms, such as agreements, contracts, or licenses, already exist. Others, such as compulsory licenses at an international level, do not currently exist. For each of these mechanisms, please indicate whether your agency would support or oppose such a mechanism by circling a number from 1 through 5. Circle a 1 if you strongly support such a mechanism, and circle a 5 if you strongly oppose such a mechanism. Use the numbers in between to express points between strong support and strong opposition, with "3" being used to express "no opinion."

Type of Control Mechanism	Strong Support		No Opinion		Strong Opposition
a) Changes in your country's copyright law so that it directly addresses the use, modification, and distribution of copyrighted computer data bases.	1	2	3	4	5
b) Limited or controlled access by means of agreements, contracts, or licenses with "user" organizations such as other national bibliographic agencies; no payment required.	1	2	3	4	5
c) Limited or controlled access by means of agreements, contracts, or licenses with "intermediary" organizations such as commercial firms which provide access to numerous data bases; payment according to amount of use.	1	2	3	4	5
d) Compulsory licensing - By international law, any organization would be allowed to use, modify, or distribute your data base upon payment of a fee or fee schedule set by an international licensing agent or organization.	1	2	3	4	5
e) Blanket license - A user or intermediary organization would negotiate with your organization the payment of a flat fee to cover moderate fluctuations in volume of use; the fee would be tied to the size or budget of the organization, rather than to the level of use.	1	2	3	4	5
f) An international clearinghouse or consortium would be empowered by its members to negotiate contracts, licenses, and fees for the bibliographic data bases which are registered with it.	1	2	3	4	5
g) No control over use, modification, or distribution; only a minimal fee would be assessed by the supplying organization to cover the cost of reproducing and delivering a data tape.	1	2	3	4	5
h) Electronic control over the on-line access to your machine-readable bibliographic records; only users authorized by your organization would be supplied with an appropriate password or access code.	1	2	3	4	5

47. Please use this page to express any further opinions or concerns you have concerning copyright, machine-readable bibliographic records, and international data flow.

APPENDIX D

INDIVIDUALS INTERVIEWED FOR THIS STUDY

INDIVIDUALS WHO WERE INTERVIEWED FOR THIS STUDY

Henriette Avram
Director, Processing Systems, Networks and Automation Planning
Library of Congress
Washington, DC 20540

Toni Carbo Bearman
Executive Director
National Commission on Libraries and Information Science
1717 K Street, N.W.
Washington, DC 20036

Bill Bucanan
Carrollton Press
1911 Ft. Myer Drive
Arlington, VA 22209

Richard M. Dougherty, Director
University of Michigan Library
Ann Arbor, MI 48109

Warren J. Haas, President
Council on Library Resources
1 Dupont Circle, N.W.
Washington, DC 20036

Joanne Harrar, Director
University Libraries
University of Maryland at College Park
College Park, MD 20742

Madeline Henderson
5021 Alta Vista Road
Bethesda MD 20014

Lee Jones
Council on Library Resources
1 Dupont Circle, N.W.
Washington, DC 20036

Michael S. Keplinger
Copyright Office
Library of Congress
1st and Independence Avenue, S.E.
Washington, DC 20540

Emery Koltay
Director, Serials Bibliography and Standards
R.R. Bowker Company
1180 Avenue of the Americas
New York, NY 10036

Joseph Kuney
Vice President
Informatics, Inc.
Rockville, MD 20852

Susan K. Martin
Director, Milton S. Eisenhower Library
Johns Hopkins University
Baltimore, MD 21218

Sandra K. Paul
SKP Associates
160 5th Avenue
New York, NY 10017

Carol Risher
Association of American Publishers
1707 L Street, N.W.
Washington, DC 20036

Edward Shaw
Research Libraries Group, Inc.
Encina Commons
Stanford University
Stanford, CA 94305

Robert Wedgeworth
Executive Director
American Library Association
50 East Huron Street
Chicago, IL 60611

Robert Willard
Information Industry Association
316 Pennsylvania Avenue, S.E.
Washington, DC 20003

James Woods
Chemical Abstracts Service
2540 Olentangy River Road
Columbus, OH 43210

Peter Young
Catalog Distribution Service
Library of Congress
Washington, DC 20540

Roderick Duschesne
National Library of Canada
395 Wellington Street
Ottawa, Ontario, Canada

APPENDIX E

INTERVIEW QUESTIONS

INTERVIEW QUESTIONS
FOR IFLA's
INTERNATIONAL STUDY OF COPYRIGHT
OF BIBLIOGRAPHIC RECORDS IN
MACHINE-READABLE FORM

1. Please describe your and your organization's role in relation to bibliographic data in machine-readable form, e.g., are you a generator, distributor, or user? (The term "bibliographic data" as used here refers primarily to library-generated data as opposed to commercially-supplied abstracting and indexing data which can be searched online.)

2. Generation of bibliographic data

   A. How, why, and to what degree, should a library or other agency which contributes bibliographic records to a machine-readable database retain control over those records? Specifically, what kinds of changes should or should not be allowed:

      - format?
      - content?
      - additions?
      - deletions?

   B. How can generators of bibliographic data receive appropriate returns on the investments they make in developing databases containing bibliographic data?

   C. Should a distinction be made between publicly-supported generators and commercial generators of bibliographic data, for example, in terms of remuneration?

   D. What kinds of costs should or should not be recovered?

   E. What kinds of changes (legal, financial, contractual, technological, or organizational) may occur over the next five years which will affect the generation of bibliographic records in machine-readable form? Over the next ten years?

3. Distribution of bibliographic data

   A. At what point or points in the distribution cycle should control be exercised over the contents of the data base?

      - input?
      - use - searching only?
      - use - creating hard copy?
      - use - redistributing? re-selling?

B. Should the protection of the data base during the distribution cycle cover -

- data base as a whole?
- individual records?
- search process?
- data elements within records?

4. Usage of bibliographic data

A. What kinds of uses are currently being made of bibliographic data available in machine-readable form?

B. Are there uses libraries or others would like to make of bibliographic data in machine-readable form but cannot because of legal, financial, contractual, technological, or organizational constraints?

C. What legal, financial, contractual, technological, or organizational changes may occur over the next five years which will affect the distribution of bibliographic records in machine-readable form? Over the next ten years?

5. Protection mechanisms

A. What criteria are most important to you in evaluating alternative mechanisms for providing protection for bibliographic records? Examples of possible criteria are:

- ability to assist in cost recovery
- simplicity of implementation
- protection of the "integrity" of individual records

B. Attached to these questions is an extract from a questionnaire, recently mailed to 35 national bibliographic agencies around the world, which asks for reactions to a set of "control-mechanisms" concerning the international exchange of bibliographic records in machine-readable form. Please react to these mechanisms in terms of your support or opposition, and make any comments you feel appropriate concerning your opinions about the international exchange of bibliographic data in machine-readable form.

C. Finally, from your own and your own organization's perspective, how major a problem is the protection of bibliographic data in machine-readable form?

SECTION 7*

MECHANISMS FOR CONTROLLING THE INTERNATIONAL DISTRIBUTION AND USE OF BIBLIOGRAPHIC RECORDS IN MACHINE-READABLE FORM

As electronic systems increase in sophistication and ease of use, it will become easier for large groups of international users to obtain access to bibliographic records in machine-readable form which are produced by organizations such as yours. Traditional mechanisms for controlling access to information, such as copyright, pricing, licensing mechanisms, and import/export laws, may need to change to accommodate changes in technology. This is especially true with regard to systems which provide on-line access on an international basis to a variety of data bases. For several years now, publishers of printed indexing and abstracting publications have been concerned that on-line access to their data bases may erode their print subscriptions. Some publishers of national bibliographies may also have similar concerns, especially since they may wish or need to recover a portion of their costs for data base development or distribution.

46. On the next page we have listed a variety of "control mechanisms" which might be proposed for controlling the international modification, distribution and use of bibliographic records in machine-readable form. Some of these mechanisms, such as agreements, contracts, or licenses, already exist. Others, such as compulsory licenses at an international level, do not currently exist. For each of these mechanisms, please indicate whether your agency would <u>support</u> or <u>oppose</u> such a mechanism by circling a number from 1 through 5. Circle a 1 if you <u>strongly support</u> such a mechanism, and circle a 5 if you <u>strongly oppose</u> such a mechanism. Use the numbers in between to express points between strong support and strong opposition, with "3" being used to express "no opinion."

*Reproduced from the IFLA Survey questionnaire for the International Study of Copyright of Bibliographic Records in Machine-Readable Form.

APPENDIX F

STUDY BIBLIOGRAPHY

BIBLIOGRAPHY

1. Avram, Henriette E. "The Impact of Technology on Legislation Affecting Libraries." IFLA Journal 6 (1980).

2. Avram, H. D. and S. E. McCallum. "Directions in Library Networking." Journal of the American Society for Information Science 31:6:438-444 (November 1980).

3. "The Berne Convention." Appendix 27. In: Nimmer On Copyright. Vol. IV. New York: Matthew Bender, 1981.

4. Brandhorst, Ted and Martha Williams. "Machine-Readable Data Bases: Copyright Status. Bulletin of the American Society for Information Science 4:4:31 (April 1978).

5. Braunstein, Yale M. et al. Economics of Property Rights As Applied to Computer Software and Data Bases. Report prepared for the National Commission on New Technological Uses of Copyrighted Works (CONTU). New York: New York University, June 1977.

6. Bush, George P. and Robert H. Dreyfuss, Eds. Technology and Copyright. Mt. Airy, Maryland: Lomond Books, 1979.

7. Carlile, Huntington. "The Diversity Among Legal Structures of Library Networks." In: Networks for Networkers. Edited by Barbara E. Markuson and Blanche Woolls. New York: Neal-Schuman Publishers, 1979.

8. Chartrand, Robert Lee and Jane Bortnick. Highlights of the White House Conference on Library and Information Services: Pre-Conference on International Information Exchange. Washington, D.C.: Library of Congress, July 1979.

9. Chartrand, Robert Lee and Jane Bortnick. International Information Exchange: A Theme Conference Summary. Report on the White House Conference on Library and Information Services: Pre-Conference Meetings on Special Themes. July 31, 1979. Washington, D.C.: National Commission on Libraries and Information Science, October 1979.

10. Committee on Scientific and Technical Information. Legal Aspects of Computerized Information Systems. Washington, D.C.: COSATI, September 1972.

11. "Copyright - The Use of Computers for the Storage and Retrieval of Protected Works." STM Newsletter, No. 48, pp. 20-22 (June 1979).

12. "Copyright - The Use of Computers for the Storage and Retrieval of Protected Works." STM Newsletter, No. 51, pp. 21-22 (January 1980).

13. Cullis, J. G. and P. A. West. "The Economics of Public Lending Right." Scottish Journal of Political Economy 24:2:169-174 (June 1977).

14. de Sangster, Mercedes Gazzolo. Legal Deposit and the Universal Availability of Publications (UAP): The Case of Peru. UFISLAA 2:1:29-34 (1980).

15. Elrod, J. McRee. "Universal Availability of Bibliographic Records." IFLA Journal 4:4:347-350 (1978).

16. Epstein, H. "Network Technology Today." Journal of the American Society for Information Science 31:6:425-437 (November 1980).

17. "European Data Base Market to Nearly Triple in 1980 Decade." Information Hot Line 12:11:1,11 (December 1980).

18. Freeman, Robert R., Janice Heyworth, and Allen Varley. "Development of a Policy for Access to an International Database, Aquatic Sciences and Fisheries Abstracts." In: Proceedings of the ASIS Annual Meeting 1979 Vol. 16. Edited by Roy D. Tally and Ronald R. Deultgen. White Plains, New York: American Society for Information Science, 1979.

19. Gotlieb, Allan, Charles Dalfen, and Kenneth Katz. "The Transborder Transfer of Information by Communications and Computer Systems: Issues and Approaches to Guiding Principles." American Journal of International Law 68:227-257 (1974).

20. Groenewegen, Hans W. "National and International Co-operation in the Creation of Bibliographic Networks: A Comparison of Experiences." Australian Library Journal pp. 47-53 (May 16, 1980).

21. Hanson, Arthur B. Omnibus Copyright Revision: Comparative Analysis of the Issues. Prepared by the United States Air Force, Cambridge Research Institute. Washington, D.C.: American Society for Information Science, 1973.

22. Hébert, Francoise and Wanda Noël. Copyright and Library Materials for the Handicapped. Prepared for the International Federation of Library Associations and Institutions. Toronto, Canada: Canadian National Institute for the Blind, January 1981.

23. Hill, M.W. and J.D. Ross. "Interaction with National and International Library Resources." In: Developing Library Effectiveness for the Next Decade.

24. "HR 3137 Proposes Information Policy Institute." Library Journal, pp. 1461-1466 (August 1981).

25. Hsiao, David K., Douglas S. Kerr, and Stuart E. Madnick. Computer Security. New York: Academic Press, 1979.

26. IFLA International Office for UBC. "The International Congress on National Bibliographies, Paris, 12-17 September 1977: Report and Recommendations." IFLA Journal 4:1:10-16 (1978).

27. International Access to MARC Records: A Summary Report with Recommended Text for a Bilateral Agreement for the International Exchange of MARC Records. IFLA International Office for UBC Occasional Papers, No. 7. London: IFLA International Office for UBC, 1980.

28. International Federation of Library Associations and Institutions. UNIMARC: Universal MARC Format. London: IFLA International Office for UBC, 1977.

29. The International MARC Network: Bibliographic Study. IFLA International Office for UBC Occasional Paper, No. 4. London: IFLA International Office for UBC, 1977.

30. Johnston, Donald F. Copyright Handbook. New York: R.R. Bowker Co., 1978.

31. Kaltwasser, Franz Georg. "The Quest for Universal Bibliographical Control." Wilson Library Bulletin, pp. 894-901 (June 1972).

32. Keplinger, Michael S. "Copyright and Information Technology." Annual Review of Information Science and Technology, Vol. 15, pp. 3-33. Edited by Martha E. Willian White Plains, New York: Knowledge Industry Publications, 1980.

33. Kilgour, Frederick G. "Increased UAP Effected by an On-Line Union Catalog." Interlending Review 7:1:20-22 (1979).

34. Library of Congress. Copyright and the Librarian. Circular R21. Washington, D.C.: U.S. Government Printing Office, 1977.

35. Line, Maurice. "Universal Availability of Publications: Progress and Development." IFLA Journal 4:4:345-346 (1978),

36. Marshall, Nancy H. "Copyright." In: The ALA Yearbook 1980. Edited by Robert Wedgeworth. Chicago: American Library Association, 1980.

37. Massil, S. Resource Sharing for National Bibliographic Services. Report of the International Congress on National Bibliographies, Paris, September 12-15, 1977. Paris: Unesco, 1977.

38. Miller, Elizabeth K. and Kate Wild. "A Strategy for International Information Systems." Special Libraries 69:435-442 (November 1978).

39. "A Nationwide Network: Development, Governance, Support." Discussion paper resulting from a meeting held by the Library of Congress Network Advisory Committee, October 1-2, 1980. Washington, D.C.: Library of Congress, December 1980.

40. Network Advisory Committee. Minutes of Meeting, March 4-5, 1980.

41. Nicholas, Henry. Copyright-Information Technology-Public Policy Part I: Copyright-Public Policies. New York: Marcel Dekker, Inc., 1975.

42. Nicholas, Henry. Copyright-Information Technology-Public Policy Part II: Public Policies-Information Technology. New York: Marcel Dekker, Inc., 1976.

43. Organization for Economic Cooperation and Development. Information Computer Communications Policy, 2: The Usage of International Data Networks in Europe. Paris: OECD, 1979.

44. Pomassl, Gerhard. "IFLA and International Bibliographical Activities (1966-1976)." Herald of Library Science 17:2-3:172-181 (April-July 1978).

45. Popov, Vladimir. "The Feasibility of an International Multilateral UNESCO Convention on the Universal Availability of Publications." Paper presented at the 45th Conference of the International Federation of Library Associations and Institutions, Copenhagen, Denmark, August 27-September 1, 1979.

46. "Resource Sharing in Asia and Oceania." IFLA Journal 5:4:337-340 (1979).

47. Robinson, B.M. "Cooperation and Competition Among Library Networks." Journal of the American Society for Information Science 31:6:413-424 (November 1980).

48. Rodriguez, Adolfo. "Universal Availability of Publications in Developing Countries." Interlending Review 6:3:90-92 (1978).

49. Saltman, Roy G. Computer Science and Technology: Copyright in Computer-Readable Works: Policy Impacts of Technological Change. Washington, D.C.: National Bureau of Standards, October 1977.

50. Squires, Jeffrey. "Copyright and Compilations in the Computer Era: Old Wine in New Bottles." Bulletin of the Copyright Society of the U.S.A. 24:1:18-46 (October 1976).

51. Stevens, N.D. "Library Networks and Resource Sharing in the United States: An Historical and Philosophical Overview." Journal of the American Society for Information Science 31:6:405-412 (November 1980).

52. "Testimony of Peter F. Urbach." Copyright Office Hearing. New York, January 8, 1981.

53. "Universal Copyright Convention." Appendix 25. In: Nimmer on Copyright. Vol. IV. New York: Matthew Bender, 1981.

54. Urquhart, D.J. "UAP: What can we do about it?" IFLA Journal 4:4:338-344 (1978).

55. U.S. Congress. House. Committee on Government Operations. International Data Flow: hearings before the Subcommittee on Government Information and Individual Rights of the House Committee on Government Operations. 96th Congress, 2nd Session, 1980. Washington: U.S. Government Printing Office, 1980.

56. Veith, Richard H. "Transborder Data Traffic: U.S. Unpredictability is Unsettling." Bulletin of the American Society for Information Science 5:6:24-25 (August 1979).

57. Vickers, Stephen C.J. "Universal Availability of Publications - A Bibliography." IFLA Journal 6:1:22-25 (1980).

58. Webster, Duane E. and Lenore S. Maruyama. "Ownership and Distribution of Bibliographic Data: Highlights of A Meeting Held by the Library of Congress Network Advisory Committee." Washington, D.C.: Library of Congress, December 1980.

59. Wells, A. J. "The International MARC Network: A Study for An International Bibliographic Data Network." The IFLA Office for UBC Occasional Papers, No. 3. London: IFLA Office for UBC, 1977.

60. White, Peter. "Privacy--An International Concern." International Library Review 12:223-242 (1980).

61. Wijasuriya, D.E.K. "IFLA's Programmes for Bibliographic Control and Developing Country Priorities." IFLA Journal 3:3:251-257 (1977).

62. Wilcox, Alice E. "Copyright." In: The ALA Yearbook 1979. Edited by Robert Wedgeworth. Chicago: American Library Association, 1979.

63. World Intellectual Property Organization. Model Provisions on the Protection of Computer Software. Report No. 64. Geneva, Switzerland: WIPO, 1978.

64. Wysocki, A. "International Co-operation in Information Transfer." Journal of Documentation 34:4:300-310 (December 1978).

65. Young, Mary E. Copyrights, 1964-May 1980. Citations from the NTIS Data Base. Springfield, Virginia: National Technical Information Service, June 1980. (PB80-810823).

International Federation of Library Associations and Institutions

Series IFLA Publications

Edited by Willem R. H. Koops

1 **Special Libraries – Worldwide.** A collection of papers prepared for the Section of Special Libraries of the International Federation of Library Associations. Edited by Günther Reichardt. 1974. 360 pages. Bound. DM 68.00, IFLA members DM 51.00. ISBN 3-7940-4421-5

2 **National Library Buildings.** Proceedings of a colloquium held in Rome, 3–6 September 1973. Edited by Anthony Thompson. 1975. 144 pages. Bound DM 28.00, IFLA members DM 21.00. ISBN 3-7940-4422-3

3 **Le Contrôle bibliographique dans les pays en développement.** Table ronde sur le contrôle bibliographique universel dans les pays en développement, Grenoble, 22–25 août 1973. Edité par Marie-Louise Bossuat, Geneviéve Feuillebois, Monique Pelletier. 1975. 165 pages. Relié. DM 38.00, pour membres d'IFLA DM 29.00. ISBN 3-7940-4423-1

4 **National and International Library Planning.** Key papers presented at the 40th Session of the IFLA General Council, Washington, D.C. 1974. Edited by Robert Vosper and Leone I. Newkirk. 1976. 162 pages. Bound. DM 38.00, IFLA members DM 29.00. ISBN 3-7940-4424-X

5 **Reading in a Changing World.** Papers presented at the 38th Session of the IFLA General Council, Budapest, 1972. Edited by Foster E. Mohrhardt. 1976. 134 pages. Bound. DM 28.00, IFLA members DM 21.00. ISBN 3-7940-4425-8

6 **The Organization of the Library Profession.** A symposium based on contributions to the 37th Session of the IFLA General Council, Liverpool, 1971. Edited by A. H. Chaplin. 1976. 2nd edition. 132 pages. Bound. DM 28.00, IFLA members DM 21.00. ISBN 3-7940-4309-X

7 **World Directory of Administrative Libraries.** A guide of libraries serving national, state, provincial, and Länder-bodies, prepared for the Sub-Section of Administrative Libraries. Edited by Otto Simmler. 1976. 474 pages. Bound. DM 60.00, IFLA members DM 45.00. ISBN 3-7940-4427-4

8 **World Directory of Map Libraries.** Compiled by the Section of Geography and Map Libraries. Edited by John A. Wolter and David K. Carrington. New edition. 1983. Approx. 350 pages. Bound approx. DM 48.00, IFLA members approx. DM 36.00. ISBN 3-598-20374-8

9 **Standards for Public Libraries.** Prepared by the IFLA Section of Public Libraries. 1977. 2nd corrected edition, 53 pages. Bound DM 16.80, IFLA members DM 12.60. ISBN 3-7940-4429-0

10 **IFLA's First Fifty Years.** Achievement and challenge in international librarianship. Edited by Willem R. H. Koops and Joachim Wieder. 1977. 158 pages. Bound. DM 36.00, IFLA members DM 27.00. ISBN 3-7940-4430-4

11 **The International Federation of Library Associations and Institutions: A selected list of references.** Edited by Edward P. Cambio. 1977. 2nd revised and expanded edition. VI, 51 pages. DM 16.80, IFLA members DM 12.60. ISBN 3-7940-4431-2

12 **Library Service to Children: An International Survey.** Edited for the Section of Children's Libraries by Colin Ray. New edition. 1983. Approx. 158 pages. Approx. DM 36.00, IFLA members approx. DM 27.00. ISBN 3-7940-4432-0

13 **Allardyce, Alex: Letters for the International Exchange of Publications.** A guide to their composition in English, French, German, Russian, Spanish. Edited by Peter Genzel. 1978. 148 pages. Bound. DM 36.00, IFLA members DM 27.00. ISBN 3-7940-4433-9

14 **Resource Sharing of Libraries in Developing Countries.** Proceedings of the 1977 IFLA/UNESCO pre-session seminar for librarians from developing countries, Antwerp University, August 30–September 4, 1977. Edited by H. D. L. Vervliet. 1979. 286 pages. Bound. DM 36.00, IFLA members DM 27.00. ISBN 3-598-20375-6

15 **Libraries for All / Bibliothèques pour tous.** A World of Books and their Readers / Le monde du livre et de ses lecteurs. Papers presented at the IFLA 50th Anniversary World Congress, Brussels 1977. Edited by Robert Vosper and Willem R. H. Koops. 1980. 163 pages. Bound. DM 36.00, IFLA members DM 27.00. ISBN 3-598-20376-4

16 Library Service for the Blind and Physically Handicapped: An International Approach. Key Papers presented at the IFLA Conference, Štrbské Pleso, ČSSR. 1978. Edited by Frank Kurt Cylke. 1979. 106 pages. Bound. DM 30.00, IFLA members DM 22.50. ISBN 3-598-20377-2

17 Guide to the Availability of Theses. Compiled by the Section of University Libraries and other General Research Libraries. Edited by D. H. Borchardt and J. D. Thawley. 1981. 443 pages. Bound. DM 68.00, IFLA members DM 51.00. ISBN 3-598-20378-0

18 Studies on the International Exchange of Publications. Edited by P. Genzel. 1981. 125 pages. Bound. DM 32.00, IFLA members DM 24.00. ISBN 3-598-20379-9

19 Public Library Policy. Proceedings of the IFLA/UNESCO pre-session Seminar, Lund, Sweden August, 20–24, 1979. Edited by K. C. Harrison. 1981. 152 pages. Bound. DM 36.00, IFLA members DM 27.00. ISBN 3-598-20380-2

20 Library Education Programmes in Developing Countries with Special Reference to Asia. Proceedings of the Unesco/IFLA Pre-Conference Seminar, Manila, Philippines, 15–19 August 1980. Edited by Russell Bowden. 1982. 211 pages. Bound. DM 68.00, IFLA members DM 58.00. ISBN 3-598-20387-7

21 Françoise Hébert and Wanda Noël: Copyright and Library Materials for the Handicapped. A study prepared for the International Federation of Library Associations and Institutions. 1982. 111 pages. Bound. DM 36.00, IFLA members DM 27.00. ISBN 3-598-20381-0

22 Education of School Librarians for Central America and Panama: Some Alternatives. Papers presented at the Unesco/IFLA Seminar, San José, Costa Rica, 3–8 December 1978. Edited by Sigrun Klara Hannesdóttir. 1982. IV, 122 pages. Bound. DM 36.00, IFLA members DM 27.00 ISBN 3-598-20384-5

23 Library Service for the Blind and Physically Handicapped: An International Approach. Vol. 2. Edited by Bruce E. Massis. 1982. 123 pages. Bound. DM 32.00, IFLA members DM 24.00. ISBN 3-598-20385-3

24 Library Interior Layout and Design. Proceedings of the Seminar held in Frederiksdal, Denmark, June 16–20, 1980. Edited by Rolf Fuhlrott and Michael Dewe. 1982. 135 pages. Bound. DM 64.00, IFLA members DM 48.00. ISBN 3-598-20386-1

25 Maurice B. Line and Stephen Vickers: **Universal Availability of Publications.** 1983. 139 p. Bound. DM 42.00, IFLA members DM 31.50 ISBN 3-598-20387-X

26 David Overton: **Planning the Administrative Library.** 1983. 264 p. Bound. DM 48.00, IFLA members DM 36.00 ISBN 3-598-20388-8

27 Dennis D. McDonald, Eleanor J. Rodger and Jeffrey L. Squires: **International Study of Copyright of Bibliographic Records in Machine-readable Form.** A report prepared for the International Federation of Library Associations and Institutions. 1983. 149 p. Bound. DM 42.00, IFLA members DM 31.50 ISBN 3-598-20393-4

In preparation

28 Library Work for Children and Young Adults. Edited by Geneviève Patte. 1983. ISBN 3-598-20389-6

29 Directory of Art Libraries. Edited by Jacqueline Viaux. 1983. Approx.400 p. ISBN 3-598-20382-9

30 Manuel for Map Librarians. Edited by Hans van de Waal. 1983. Approx. 300 p. ISBN 3-598-20390-X

K · G · SAUR München · New York · London · Paris
POB 71 10 09 – D-8000 München 71 – Tel. (089) 79 89 01 – Telex 5212067 saur d